D0874361

What Others Have Said About

THE CAPITAL CAFÉ
Poems of Redneck, U.S.A.

The poems in *The Capital Café* tell stories, but they are not narrative poems. They have incidents rather than plots and ruminations rather than dramatic climaxes. And though there is some passage of time, the poems really exist all at once, portraying every nuance of two small communities organically and simultaneously. Brodsky's influences are many, from the Greek poets to Swift to Faulkner. But for me, *The Capital Café* reveals small town life with the same intimacy and moral purpose as Sherwood Anderson.
— Gregory Curtis, Editor of The 1991 National Magazine Award-winning *Texas Monthly*

Brodsky's minutely observed café society is funny, intense, tragic, vaguely sinister, and disturbingly familiar. The poetry resounds because "Redneck, U.S.A." is not limited to the Deep South; it can be found in any geographical clime, even where you live. *Especially* where you live.
— Tom Dupree, Senior Editor, Bantam Books

The Capital Café, by Louis Daniel Brodsky, reflects a Jewish sense of alienation, of being a stranger in a strange land, but more than that, it allows the reader to see the truest versions of America. Brodsky's characters lift up the skirts of the Klan and peek underneath. This is a risky book. Beneath the steaming grits and biscuits and gravy, Brodsky reveals startling visions of redneck America that not only exist in Missouri but in every state of this fair nation.
— Adrian C. Louis, author of *Among the Dog Eaters*

Louis Daniel Brodsky's poetry has reached new heights in *The Capital Café*, etching vivid portraits of small town Americans in middle America. He has captured all our lives in these stunning poems, extending the range across all world boundaries with classical, Biblical and literary allusions woven into the fabric of his stunning tapestry. His characters come alive in the collective consciousness of anyone who has traveled through the heartland of bigotry, the wasteland of prejudice, the fog-bound lowlands of ignorance, the tangled brushlands where zealots scream for blood. Writing with controlled passion, Brodsky has mapped two Missouri towns with a lyrical intensity that transcends language, speech, giving us a holy chant, a song of people trapped in the terrible blindness that afflicts only those who will not see. In Brodsky's deft hands, that chant soars above anger and fury into a brilliant song that will echo in the heart of the reader long after the book is closed.

— Jory Sherman, author of the Golden Spur Award-winning *The Medicine Horn*

The Capital Café is a collection of poems about Redneck, U.S.A. But where, geographically, is Redneck, U.S.A.? Traditionally, one thinks of the South or the Midwest. And though L.D. Brodsky's book is set, in the first part, in a bedroom community of St. Louis and, in the second, a farming community in a more rural part of Missouri, readers who see themselves therein realize that Redneck, U.S.A., isn't as much a geographic location as it is a state of being. The Capital Cafés of the story could be in New York, Chicago, Seattle, Dallas, or Sardis, Mississippi.

The work is, in the first half, a slice of life observed by Moe Fischer, formerly a high-school English teacher, now a proofreader for the local newspaper, but always a voyeur, an oral historian, and a Jew, adrift in a belt of Baptist piety. In the second half, it is a mosaic seen by rural Americans in seed caps,

> *Green-billed, red-meshed, and blue-ribbed,*

exemplified by the Holsum Bread man, winking furtively at the Reverend Bone's eighteen-year-old daughter,

> *. . . Helen, the teenage waitress of local breeding,*
> *Who's stuffed into tight jeans . . .*

If, one hundred years from now, researchers want to find the "voice" of mid-twentieth-century America's Heartland, they need go no further than L.D. Brodsky's *The Capital Café*. Mr. Brodsky writes for the ear, the soul, and the gut. No iambic pentameter this; his poems aren't watercress sandwiches and petits fours for the Sunday afternoon library guild. They are

> *. . . sizzling ham steaks and bacon*
> *Twitching on a scorching griddle . . .*

for the six a.m. breakfast crowd: the Chevy-Buick dealer, the undertaker, the deputy sheriff, the waitress, and the roller-rink owner.

The Capital Café would more accurately be called a poetic book rather than a book of poetry, for each poem builds upon the others like chapters in an engrossing novel. Brodsky writes in a style that resonates through the reader's soul. The alliteration, the pacing, and the music of his poetry are uniquely his own, yet so familiar is the imagery that the reader is almost convinced that he isn't reading it at all but merely remembering his own past.

L.D. Brodsky's powerful writing has broken poetry free from convention. He is, quite simply, one of America's very best.

— Robert Vaughan, author of *The American Chronicles*

The Capital Café

Poems of Redneck, U.S.A.

Books by
LOUIS DANIEL BRODSKY

Poetry
Trilogy: A Birth Cycle   (1974)
Monday's Child   (1975)
The Kingdom of Gewgaw   (1976)
Point of Americas II   (1976)
Preparing for Incarnations   (1976)
La Preciosa   (1977)
Stranded in the Land of Transients   (1978)
The Uncelebrated Ceremony of Pants Factory Fatso   (1978)
Birds in Passage   (1980)
Résumé of a Scrapegoat   (1980)
Mississippi Vistas: Volume One of *A Mississippi Trilogy*   (1983) (1990)
You Can't Go Back, Exactly   (1988)
The Thorough Earth   (1989)
Four and Twenty Blackbirds Soaring   (1989)
Falling from Heaven: Holocaust Poems of a Jew and a Gentile
   (with William Heyen)   (1991)
Forever, for Now: Poems for a Later Love   (1991)
Mistress Mississippi: Volume Three of *A Mississippi Trilogy*   (1992)
A Gleam in the Eye: Poems for a First Baby   (1992)
Gestapo Crows: Holocaust Poems   (1992)
The Capital Café: Poems of Redneck, U.S.A.   (1993)

Bibliography (Coedited with Robert Hamblin)
Selections from the William Faulkner Collection of Louis Daniel Brodsky:
   A Descriptive Catalogue   (1979)
Faulkner: A Comprehensive Guide to the Brodsky Collection
      Volume I: The Biobibliography   (1982)
      Volume II: The Letters   (1984)
      Volume III: The De Gaulle Story   (1984)
      Volume IV: Battle Cry   (1985)
      Volume V: Manuscripts and Documents   (1989)
Country Lawyer and Other Stories for the Screen by William
   Faulkner   (1987)
Stallion Road: A Screenplay by William Faulkner   (1989)

Biography

William Faulkner, Life Glimpses   (1990)

The Capital Café
Poems of Redneck, U.S.A.

by

Louis Daniel Brodsky

TIME BEING BOOKS®
POETRY IN SIGHT AND SOUND

Time Being Books®
10411 Clayton Road
St. Louis, Missouri 63131

Time Being Books® volumes are printed on acid-free paper, and binding materials are chosen for strength and durability.

Time Being Books® is an imprint of Time Being Press, Inc., St. Louis, Missouri, and is registered in the U.S. Patent and Trademark Office.

ISBN 1-877770-48-5
ISBN 1-877770-49-3 (pbk.)
ISBN 1-877770-51-5 (cassette)

Library of Congress Cataloging-in-Publication Data

Brodsky, Louis Daniel.
    The Capital Café : poems of redneck, U.S.A. / by Louis Daniel Brodsky.
        p.   cm.
    ISBN 1-877770-48-5 (cloth) : $18.95. — ISBN 1-877770-49-3 (paper) : $12.95   CIP
    1. City and town life — Missouri — Poetry. I. Title.
PS3511.A86C36   1993
811'.54—dc20   93-24238

Cover design by Tony Tharenos
Book design by Lori Loesche
Manufactured in the United States of America

First Edition, first printing (December 1993)

Acknowledgments

The earliest of these poems, "Out of the Cradle, Endlessly Grousing," was written July 21, 1972; the latest, *Miss Missouri,*" was composed September 29, 1989. Four of them, "Running in Packs," "The Isle of Lesbos," "The Auction," and "Helen Among the 12 Disciples," originally appeared in different versions in *Four and Twenty Blackbirds Soaring* (St. Louis: Timeless Press, 1989). The last of these four originally carried the following dedication: "For Margaret and Dick Haxel." I express my thanks to Time Being Press, Inc., for permission to reprint these poems.

I extend my appreciation to the following magazines, in which some of these poems, in different versions, have appeared or will appear: *Amelia* ("Helen Among the 12 Disciples" and "The Isle of Lesbos"); Ball State University's *Forum* ("Running in Packs"); and *Sparrow* ("Out of the Cradle, Endlessly Grousing").

For their valuable editorial assistance, my appreciation goes to Senior Editor Jerry Call, Editors Sheri Vandermolen and Lori Loesche, of Time Being Books, and to Adrian C. Louis, who read an early version of this book and made a number of recommendations.

Grateful acknowledgement is made for use of certain passages from *The Sound and the Fury,* by William Faulkner. Copyright © 1929 and renewed 1957 by William Faulkner. Reprinted by permission of Random House, Inc.

To Dick Vaughan,
dear friend and revered author,
I humbly dedicate this account
of my Travels
into Several Remote Nations
of the World.

Contents

LAPINGA, MO.
Pop. 10,001

LAPUTA, MO.
Pop. (est.) 2119

The Capital Café

Poems of Redneck, U.S.A.

He likewise directed, that every senator in the great council of a nation, after he had delivered his opinion, and argued in the defence of it, should be obliged to give his vote directly contrary; because if that were done, the result would infallibly terminate in the good of the public.

* * *

It is likewise to be observed, that this society hath a peculiar cant and jargon of their own, that no other mortal can understand, and wherein all their laws are written, which they take special care to multiply; whereby they have wholly confounded the very essence of truth and falsehood, of right and wrong; . . .

— from *Gulliver's Travels*, Jonathan Swift

Lapinga, Mo.

Pop. 10,001

About that time Earl started yelling at Job, so I put them away and went over to try to put some life into him. What this country needs is white labour. Let these damn trifling niggers starve for a couple of years, then they'd see what a soft thing they have.

* * *

"I've known some jews that were fine citizens. You might be one yourself," I says.

"No," he says, "I'm an American."

"No offense," I says. "I give every man his due, regardless of religion or anything else. I have nothing against jews as an individual," I says. "It's just the race. You'll admit that they produce nothing. They follow the pioneers into a new country and sell them clothes."

"You're thinking of Armenians," he says, "aren't you. A pioneer wouldn't have any use for new clothes."

"No offense," I says. "I dont hold a man's religion against him."

"Sure," he says, "I'm an American. My folks have some French blood, why I have a nose like this. I'm an American, all right."

"So am I," I says. "Not many of us left."

— from ***The Sound and the Fury***, William Faulkner

City of Traditional Progress

They refer to this small town, Lapinga,
Cradled in the Ozark foothills
Just an hour-plus commute southwest from St. Louis,
As a "bedroom community,"
"A nice place to retire to"
(Nobody bothers to lock his car or house),
A "Five-Star" designee by the state's Bureau of Tourism,
Whose motto, "City of Traditional Progress,"
On the sun-faded, ramshackle, 10' x 40' billboard
Stranded back in a cornfield off Highway 69
Like an abandoned manure spreader,
Can barely be read anymore
From vehicles speeding down to Arkansas and Tennessee.

Sociologists ranging out to drill cores,
Take soundings and fallout readings,
Need go no farther than the Capital Café
To glean oral evidence
Of how easily provoked is public indignation
By such sore spots and open wounds
As bigotry, racism, complacence, mendacity,
Chauvinism, hypocrisy, vanity,
And inflexible, fanatical religiosity;
Each citizen is an exemplar of jingoistic Americanism,
Christian morality
With an old-rugged-cross bias
Toward Fundamentalist Baptist exclusivity.

"A great place to raise your kids up"
Permeates Lions, Masons, and Elks rhetoric,
Chamber of Commerce and Kiwanis antiphons and litanies;
It's drifted for so long off tongue-tips
Of everyone afraid to extricate his head
From the ostrich-hole he's dug over the decades
That now, saying "ain't"s and "don't"s,
Doing "the nasty" and drugs in grade school,
And eschewing even a junior-college education
To stay home and take up the family "operation"
Have become the enduring qualifications
For maintaining the town's proud self-image,
Perpetuating the sweetest way of life on God's green earth.

In the Autumn of His Years

A retiree from St. Louis to this "bedroom community,"
I, Moses Fischer, better known as Moe,
Sit in the Capital Café this 6 a.m.,
Witnessing regulars, strays, outpatients (no women welcomed)
Come to partake of coffee and conversation
Ranging from the World Series
To the latest "inside trader" information
On the volatility of stock exchanges
In London, Sydney, Hong Kong, Tokyo, and New York;
Here in Lapinga, where the word "Recession"
Has been deleted from the indigenous vocabulary,
Anyone reported resorting to such sordid rumors
Will be shot dead on the spot, then arrested
By Deputy Sheriff Leroy "Butch" Wampler himself.

Reversing my role, this past decade,
As a former high-school English teacher,
I've attended classes here in Lapinga's "School of Athens,"
Taking notes on its professors' conventional wisdom,
Aphorisms, cynical vituperations,
And humorous solutions to cosmic conundrums,
Local politics, and Sphinx-like social and emotional enigmas
Igniting with each spark from their flinty tongues.
In my self-appointed role as student sociologist
Of this mid-Missouri town of ten thousand and one souls,
I've never considered myself an eavesdropper
Or voyeur but rather an oral historian
With a high-priority mission to fix for posterity
The lexical treasures of this thriving, if remote, nation.

It may be pure invention or latent paranoia,
But some days I sense their tolerance of my presence
Straining to the breaking point.
Recently I've seen them whispering, grimacing,
Casting scrutinizing eyes in my direction,
Felt vague traces of hatred surfacing,
Reinforcing doubts about my neutral status
Amidst this working-class caste
*

That convenes daily across from the Courthouse
To impose Mores, Myth, History, and Fate
On everyone within earshot's constricted radius.
This morning, their religious disquisition,
Blatantly racist in its Baptist piety,
Drifts toward me like Hiroshima fallout.

Unequivocally, they've concluded
That last week's Black Friday stock-market debacle
Was "Jew-manipulated"
And that I, being the nearest "kike,"
Not to mention one of only two they know
(They don't consider my wife human either)
Or, for that matter, have ever even seen close up,
Am, by default, "un-American,"
A McCarthy-listed threat to their very existences.
Anxious, I refuse Sue's newest coffee offering,
Instead signal for my check,
Pay, then exit the café into sunshine,
Praying that, somehow, at least this crisp October day
Will respect the Jew in me I can't deny.

Moe's Bone of Contention

Billowing, acrid smoke,
Thick from sizzling ham steaks and bacon
Twitching on a scorching griddle,
Fills this seedy café
Early this sunny, autumnal Monday morning,
Through whose chill I've just bristled
To order breakfast and listen to "ain't"s,
"Smack-dab"s, and "hot-damn" politics
Scratch down the blackboard
Of my barely awakened imagination
Before heading to the *Lapinga Bugle* office,
Where I volunteer two days a week
Reading copy just to keep my mind alert.

Buick dealer, newly elected Deputy Sheriff,
Undertaker, City Attorney,
Various farmers, fakers, faith healers,
Local franchisees of Ben Franklin, Gambles,
Sonic, Western Auto, Radio Shack,
Pizza Hut, MFA, and IGA,
And the most recent owner of Nick's Liquors
Invoke rain, sleet, snow, tornado, drought, plague,
Tidal wave, hurricane, erupting volcano
To effect measures necessary for restraining free trade
Through loss-leader advertising,
Price fixing, downright lying —
Their own parochial brand of laissez faire.

Cigar, pipe, and unfiltered cigarette fumes
Further foul the air
Inside this greasy amphitheater,
Like cars bumper-locked for miles on a freeway,
Giving off nauseating exhaust.
My pained eyes, complaining crazily,
Squint a headache into existence
As they gaze straight ahead
Past the flaking, gold-leaf letters
*

— CAPITAL CAFÉ —

Amateurishly reverse-painted on the plate glass.
Slowly, four fluted columns
Of the slate-gray Courthouse come into focus.

Something in the opaque smoke
Disposes me to skeptical speculation
About this pseudo-neoclassical Greek temple,
Surmounted by harpylike pigeons,
Stuck *in medias res* in dead Downtown.
Suddenly it becomes a Calvary,
And I recognize these citizens surrounding me:
Once upon another dream
They at least tolerated my people,
Jews dispersed throughout the Roman Empire,
Until one hung His son, my brother,
And all of us were implicated in that crucifixion,
Though the Gentile has yet to confess his sin.

Our Town: An Acrid Approximation

As usual, they gather in motley disarray
Weekdays and Saturdays at the Capital Café:
Merchants, purveyors, attendants, clerks,
Renters, independent operators, franchisees,
Agents, dealers, sales reps, brokers,
And all derelicts and malingerers collectively listed
By the Chamber of Commerce as "Businessmen."
They cluster like buzzards about a carcass
To conceive new absolutes and proclaim final say-sos,
Dictate obligatory mandates on Congressional debates,
Sandlot baseball, town-hall politics,
And the fate of maidenhead, motherhood, and apple pie;
Like pigeons and squirrels,
They flit from vulgarity to calumniation
As though each guffaw were a limb, ledge, eave;
Like chimpanzees discovering erogenous zones
And sexual mechanisms for the first time,
Oblivious of embarrassment public exposure creates,
They prate, stomp, beat their chests,
Bang, slap, grasp the table in oratorical attitudes
Redolent of the Three Stooges,
Tarzan, the Keystone Kops, and Ralph Kramden.

Some days, when I come downtown
To patronize Cox's Office Supply,
Jekyll's Jewelry Shop, Carter's Artificial Flowers,
Barber Dubart, Scruggs the druggist, or grocer Snell,
Or to make a return for credit at Gambles,
I can't dissociate the image of each face
Imprinted from too many early a.m.'s
We've spent in "separate-but-equal" contiguity
Within the Capital Café,
Where I go regularly to compose my thoughts
Into subliminal Op-Eds and human-interest stories,
Forge jeremiads in morning's metaphorical cauldron;
I see them smiling behind their counters,
Squirrels, buzzards, pigeons, and chimpanzees,
*

Their visages, anyway, mounted atop shoulders
Of the town's venerable patricians,
Giza-Sphinxes, Minotaurs, satyrs, Pans,
Their half-man, half-beast bodies
Reflecting age-old dichotomies,
Not the traditional opposites of head and heart,
Spirit and flesh, but rather biological differences
Between species within the same venal genus.

With taciturnity, we exchange legal tender
For goods and services rendered,
Massage our intercourse with superficial pleasantries,
Knowing we must coexist for survival:
Retired schoolteacher from the "big city"
With "all that highfalutin' education"
And homegrown "country boys made good,"
Coevals in a community too slowly expanding
For distinctions in speech patterns, dialects, vocabulary,
Aesthetics, and religious beliefs to go unnoticed.
For now, we've achieved a tenuous equilibrium:
We're at impasse. Both sides realize
That if there were a way for them to disfranchise me
Without disturbing, even to a small degree,
The town's balance of trade and GNP
And for me, with specific citations,
To indict them in *Bugle* editorials I'll never write,
Criticizing piety, racial bias,
Unbowdlerized obscenity, and self-aggrandizement,
We would each accomplish the other's demise;
But coexistence is society's solution
For preventing the fruition of human perfection.

Six mornings a week, they gather to chew the fat;
I come to listen and jot notes.
The days are fun-house mirrors
Into which we stare,
Witnessing our lives parade in distorted review —
Layers growing brittle, flaking,
*

Occasionally revealing our trivial shapes
As changeless mutations
Moving from Babel through Limbo toward Sheol,
Across the rivers Lethe and Styx in Hades,
Where Satan waits to assimilate all our voices
In one abysmal Collective Unconscious,
In which hissing and roaring form the Esperanto
Necessary for getting the business of forgetting done
Once and for all: a mighty fortress
Whose halls resound with raucous guffaws and profanations
Reminiscent of bullshit sessions in the Capital Café
In the heart of the U.S. of A., Lapinga, Mo.,
That microcosm of Life on the planet Earth,
That Eden, that green, regal realm,
That pendent orb, that Grand Experiment
God thought He'd failed to record for posterity.

Jekyll the Jeweler Suffers a Breakdown

These days, he breathes less easily
Although relieved of every responsibility except one:
He remains accountable for his freedom,
Which, before his involuntary retirement from life,
Held itself reasonably in check
With strenuous work schedules
He zealously imposed upon his perfectionistic self,
Keeping personal liberty recessive
While ambitiousness dominated his visions of success.

These days, he pursues reflections of passing cars
In windows of the hardware store, grocery, and bar
Facing Freedom and Liberty streets,
Loses count of circumnavigations he makes
Pacing around the gray granite Courthouse,
Pretending to be an intrepid English sea dog
Besting treacherous shoals
Off Capes Horn, Hatteras, and Good Hope
Or St. Francis baptizing each pigeon that crosses his path.

These days, he pours free time
From a magician's bottomless Chinese teapot
By fingering its minuscule hole
To regulate flow: despite his "affliction,"
He knows those who've witnessed his downfall
See him as just another "nigger" or "nettlesome Jew,"
Not as a former well-to-do businessman, church deacon,
C of C, Kiwanis, Elks, Lions, and Masons member,
Hail-fellow well met, Capital Café regular.

These days of his twilight,
When dusk and dawn are caught in a revolving door
He needs to squeeze through
Each morning in order to escape Sleep's corridors,
Freedom he once considered his best friend
For its deference to his aggressive obsessiveness
Has become his archnemesis. Seated on a bench,
Elbows on knees, he leans suicidally toward the street,
Breathing in exhaust, lost in ostrich-reveries.

Travels into Several Remote Nations

Breakfast at the Capital Café isn't tea and crumpets,
Nor is it grabbing on the run
A wrapped danish and acrid black coffee
Sloshing inside its capped styrofoam container
In the lobby of the New York Hilton,
Where, for three days, I stayed with my wife,
Attending the MLA Convention
Just to keep in touch with deconstructionism
And other ephemeral trends in my former profession.

In fact, today, these regulars' easy attitudes,
So starkly contrasted with the Association's sycophancy,
Pedantry, sophistry, condescension,
Studied-slovenly dress, and obsessive competitiveness,
Attest to the axiomatic socioeconomic hypotheses
That Man can adapt to castles and dung heaps
And develop characteristics specially fitted for existence
In Royal Academies on flying islands
As well as at "Country Days" pig roasts and church raffles.

Yesterday, in Manhattan, a Puerto Rican waitress,
Cursing the universe defined by the tiny space
Behind the counter confining her to the daily slavery
Of taking "What'll-it-be"s, fetching meals, humoring cooks,
Clearing dirty dishes, returning complaints
With acrimonious hostility (in Spanish),
Transliterating propositions into sign language,
Thumb-biting, and middle-finger exercises,
Her lips silently mouthing "Fuck you"s,

Spilled eggs down my shirt, on my pant legs,
Then, without apologizing, shoved a wad of napkins
In my general direction
Before spinning back to retrieve more orders.
This morning, in Lapinga, Sue's on duty,
Serving breakfast at the friendly Capital Café.
She engages in pleasant solicitudes,
Begs me to let her know if I need anything,
If the freshly brewed coffee is hot enough, the toast warm,

Whether the ham is lean;
She assures me she's personally told chef Fred
That I specifically requested Velveeta
For my four-egg "Hungry Country Boy Omelette."
A fish out of water am I, a cuckolded king,
A pariah in a Swiftian land
Upon whose shores Zephyrus has stranded my vessel,
Made me the plaything of Houyhnhnms
Who initially mistook me for a hated Yahoo

Before remanding me to my heart's own custody
And releasing my spirit to muses
Starved for the creative excesses of a retiree
Turned novice journalist, demographer, sociologist —
What a queer transmogrification
For one such as Lemuel Gulliver, alias Moe Fischer!
And yet this Midwestern Redriff,
This United Kingdom of New Jerusalem,
Suits my uprootedness, for now.

The Undertakers

For Chief Loan Officer Homer LaChance,
Each a.m. begins the same way
At the Capital Café's regulars' table,
Where he sops up homemade gravy
With buttermilk biscuits,
Crosshatches glutinous scrambled eggs
With fork and knife clicking like knitting needles,
Nibbles greasy sausage links
He lifts to his lips like Eucharist wafers,
And sips blood-rusty coffee
From a chipped Shenango china chalice
That Sue, the kitchen magician's ubiquitous assistant,
Tends to with her wandlike brew pot
While he holds forth on the latest "floating prime."

Although cynicism mixed with sardonic wit,
Homespun anecdotes, demotic puns,
Aphoristic wisdom, scatological argot,
And intermittent guffaws — always the laughter —
Are the tools these gravediggers use
To bury each other six feet under,
This morning LaChance seems a bit arthritic,
Unable to wield the bullshit shovel,
Heave his share of the dirt over his shoulder;
He seems to be getting smacked in the face
With muddy clods from all sides,
Sinking deeper and deeper in the widening mire,
Almost convinced it's he
They intend to third-mortgage, inter, and eulogize.

"How many more days, Homer?" asks barber Dubart.
"Nine," he replies with feigned reproach.
As if he's missed it, druggist Scruggs repeats,
"How many days ya got left at the bank?"
"Nine," Homer intones with growing impatience.
"I take it that includes Saturdays and Sundays,"
Pugg, the realtor, impertinently asserts,
Attempting to get LaChance's goat.
*

"That's nine *working* days until I retire,"
Homer theatrically proclaims with futile finality.
"Almost a *full* two weeks," he qualifies.
"Who they gonna get to dole out the loans,
Keep the 'conomy goin'," asks Zoren, the mortician,
"After you and the missus head off in that snazzy motor house?"

"Well, it beats the livin' hell outta me,"
Adds the Right Reverend Snavely,
"Why a man in his prime would sacrifice such a cushy job.
Everybody knows bankers are the reason
Golf courses get built."
"Boys, it's just a goddamn good thing
You ain't about to default on your notes
'Cause you can sure's hell bet 'fore I left
I'd foreclose and repossess every last red cent
You bastards own, clean down past
Your turkey-huntin', thermal-underwear asses,
Then watch you run loose as naked yahoos
Up Freedom and down Liberty streets,
Beggin' me to loan yous the shirts off my back."

"Homer, you say ya got *how many* days to go?"

Recorder of Deeds

The men enter the Capital Café
Like barracudas darting from oceanic coverts
Toward a mullet-strewn surface,
Pompous grad-school pedants
Rushing to lecture halls to intoxicate their students
With effervescent word-wine,
Field mice creeping surreptitiously
Toward rotten cheese or peanut butter
Dabbed on spring-loaded traps
Strategically located between pots and pans,
Or mongooses closing in on cobras — or vice versa.

Each morning they arrive at this polling place
In one-at-a-time droves
To register their living franchise,
Vote their identity into glib existence,
Flatulently proclaim themselves
Well-equipped to solve the Sphinx's riddle,
Advise wise Solomon,
And, through their own self-righteousness,
Confine Hadrian, Draco, and Savonarola
To lip-service posturings while espousing, unconsciously,
The teachings of Hobbes, Machiavelli, and Nietzsche.

Having long ago discovered the secret
To transforming myself on a moment's notice
From a first-person classroom moderator
Into a third-person observer,
Inconspicuous, if nominally omniscient,
I sit each morning perpetuating my anonymity,
Untouchable within my nimbus,
Listening to wisdom reproduce itself exponentially,
Trying to transcribe precisely
The geneaologies of this town's VIPs
As though my ledger were a community Bible.

Chronicling such impressive, if prolix, rhetoric,
So many impromptu speeches and diatribes,
Sermons, harangues, perorations, philippics, and jeremiads
Redolent of those delivered atop Areopagus,
From podia in Swiftian Academies on flying islands,
Matherish pulpits, *700 Club* stages,
And Congessional and Parliamentary floors,
Is not easy for an ex-English teacher
Not all that flexible of wrist
Or proficient in poeticizing flawed, fraudulent testimony
And fluent, pig-Latinish speaking in tongues.

Yet I've done it in the past,
Been assigned scribal tasks by God's apostles.
In fact, I may be the author
Not only of Deuteronomy and Psalms,
The Books of Ruth, Daniel, and the Song of Solomon,
But the Gospels, Corinthians, Thessalonians,
Ephesians, Acts, and Revelations.
Furthermore, it might have been my hand
That composed the Koran, Rig-Veda, Torah,
Kama Sutra, *Tao Te Ching*,
And those brittle Dead Sea Scrolls.

Why then, this particular morning,
My pen refuses to pursue these stupendous orators
Through their histrionic pontifications,
These canonical prelates representing civilization
Reaching beyond Epiphany toward Apotheosis,
Is impossible to assess. I do know this:
Each day I fail to record their idolatries
Creates a permanent gap in Lapinga's Golden Book.
Hopefully, God will overlook my lapses
And, come Final Judgment, accept us equally,
According to the degree of our heresies.

Rioting Heathens

Occupying this booth,
Primed to survey distant terrains
From my perch atop the earth, I wait,
Pen poised in midair
Like the axis of my spinning imagination,
Eager to see words materialize
From worlds nether and surreal,

Whirling suns, moons, and planets
Inching centripetally toward a metaphor-core
Whose aesthetic gravitational field
Will fuse all visions, prophecies, and auguries
Into a solitary revolving sphere,
A cosmic editorial, whisper of the original Whisper
Rising out of the miasmic cooling.

But the process refuses to accomplish itself;
Creation is an exercise in patience
Lacking all virtue.
The blue-ruled page remains unchanged
Despite my concentration, my ruminative gazing,
As the men at the sacrosanct back table,
Whom I'd hoped to indict,

Continue their racial vituperations unscathed,
Purging themselves with outrage
Of the curse worked by demoniac black athletes
To dominate Sunday afternoon TV,
Concluding that all "niggers" are ignorant,
Even NFL players:
"They ain't no different from a trained bird dog";

"Every last one of 'em's the same
Under them painted helmets: dumb apes
Runnin' like hell t'scape their own shadows."
My ears pulsate, but my brain
Fails to translate these stimuli into imputations
Sufficiently objectified
To evoke a publishable response. I grow tense,

Knowing I've again been defeated
In rising to my avocation of arresting Truth
Before it dissolves into its base human components
Of hypocrisy, bigotry, jealousy, piety, and lies,
Alchemizing the donkey's bray into song,
The snake's bite into a kiss, redeeming myself
By exposing these heathens to the original Whisper.

The Aldermen of Sodom & Gomorrah

On this coldest of snow-laden days,
Only the most stalwart Capital Café regulars
Summon the energy to venture out
To attend their daily convocation at the back table.

Their conversations dovetail spontaneously,
Interweave in contrapuntal fashion
Metaphysical considerations,
Predictions for summer drought, power outages,

The common drama of "busted" pipes,
Dead batteries, isolated cases of frostbite
Leading to gangrene and amputation —
A potpourri laced with select expletives

Underscoring the heavy-duty respect
These aldermanic city-fathers,
In nonacademic acquiescence, reverence,
And patriotic modesty, have for Acts of God

And other unforeseeable natural disasters
Enumerated in fine print
On homeowner's insurance policies.
All are mindful of their collective responsibility

To the constituency that narrowly elected them
Over equally indistinguishable malingerers
Desirous of adding to meager incomes
The hundred-dollar monthly dole

To sift, sort, and choose
Gratuitous gossip over fortuitous Truth;
It and Tradition have forced them to hold their meetings
In this conspicuously public location,

Where they hope to high-profile their devotion
To taking their duties to heart.
However, this morning, their insights and exhortations
Fall short of altering Fate's course,

Dissolving the frigid, gray gloom from a sky
Obviously fraught with more snow,
Or postponing indefinitely personal obligations
To show up at their places of "bidness."

Gradually, each cringes into his winter coat,
Reluctant to leave, be swallowed alive
By a 10-below beast
Zeroing in rapaciously from every direction,

Wondering now why they've even bothered
To solicit each other's wise counsel
And tried to persuade Nature
To renegotiate the dilemma of empty cash registers.

Once outside, assaying his futility
In the face of this vicious freeze,
Each alderman glances back at the Capital Café
And changes into pillar-of-the-community street salt.

Moe Sings of Cabbages and Kings

Sipping from a perpetual cup of coffee
Like a king drunk on his power,
I sit in a booth at the Capital Café,
Eager for two fried eggs, over hard,
And soggy white toast
To materialize from the spitting grill.
I needn't even raise a finger, just turn,
And one of three ladies-in-waiting
Hastens to my beck with more steaming ichor.

But I have few illusions about my suzerainty;
My influence extends only to the outermost boundaries
Of this remote inner dominion,
Camouflaged in flaking, water-stained paint
Partially concealed by contact-paper fleurs-de-lis,
Where the sky is a rusted tin ceiling
Flecked with ten fluorescent, migrainous suns,
Grease-smudged vents, grids, and ducts —
A mosaic owing its design to abject neglect.

By sight, if not by name,
I recognize ancient adversaries,
Congregated in specious debate at the back table,
Who owe no allegiance to my authority.
I pinch my cheeks to remind myself
That it takes more than imagination to defy Reality.
Yet at times even a retired high-school teacher
Yearns to rule by the divine right of kings —
Or at least by the seat of his pants.

An Unopened Gift

From my venue in this snug booth
In the Capital Café,
Looking streetward through plate glass
At the vacant Courthouse
This quiet Wednesday morning after Christ's nativity,
My mystified eyes swoop upward
And stop where roof and sky converge.

Squabs roosting in cooing ubiquity
About two inches apart
Along the eastern edge of the cornice
Form a pigeon-parapeted facade
That transports my stupefied gaze to amazement,
Stimulates my image-making apparatus
To visual epiphany.

For a moment, that seedy Greek facsimile
Is a Parthenon ornamented with caryatids,
A Renaissance cathedral
Surmounted by intricately carved steeples
Ascending in stony slenderness to God,
A Victorian Valentine's card
Laced with delicate, papery crenelations.

I blink; statuesque goddesses,
Pinnacles of divinity, origami designs
Dissolve like ice in my warm eyes.
When they refocus, a cohort of pigeons reappears,
Snowing their own blizzard of shit
Down the columns and onto steps of the Courthouse —
A Christmas gift Lapinga forgot to open.

Proclaiming an "Everlasting Yea"

Once again, like dutiful choirboys,
The men congregate to say eclectic, secular rosaries,
Make confession, perform official rituals
At the back table; they review local events,
Sort the world's metaphorical mail,
Recite the town jail's roster, sports scores,
Obituaries, marriages, public auctions, and births,
Published in Lapinga's twice-a-week "daily," the *Bugle*.
For lack of current grist,
A few refer to last week's tragedy,
Purvis Klock's suicide,
Which shocked the community, knocked down its walls
As though a conflagration or medieval plague
Had invaded its sacred precincts,
Devastated everyone with malicious efficiency;
They reprise collective sympathy and grief,
Reiterating known facts each owns
Who spoke of Purvis with fondness or deference:
"He'd been despondent ever since his wife died
Two years ago." "And that accident
This past summer — that blast to the stomach
While cleanin' his shotgun on a huntin' trip
Out at his farm — no mishap, that."
"It's all too obvious now he was practicin',
Havin' dress rehearsal, fumblin' a touchdown run."
"We shoulda realized then
He was coverin' up, shoulda guessed
He was tryin' to kill hisself and just missed."
"What a waste: them three surgeons
Stayin' up the entire night to save him . . . for this."
"I picked it up at 4:30
Last Wednesday mornin' on my police scanner;
His nearest neighbor heard the shot,
Looked out his window, and saw Purvis
Slumped on the porch like a crumpled croker sack."
"Yeh, can you 'magine?
He had to set the butt of his gun
*

Between two rabbit traps,
Jam the barrel against a busted shutter hasp . . ."
"A *what*?" "A *which*?"
"A window shutter's rusted clasp!
Then, his head pressed against the muzzle,
Usin' a rake handle to reach the trigger,
He blew his brains all over the siding."
"God, how grotesque!" "How *what*?"
"And ya know, since Opal'd passed,
He'd been to Tahoe, Reno, Barbados,
And to Canada after Kodiak."
"Yeh, I'm sure he was tryin' like crazy
To run away from his loneliness."
"He'd become despondent, they say."
"Jus' couldn't seem to find hisself in retirement."
"Yeh, sellin' the hardware store,
Then losin' Opal just months later
Musta been too much loss."
"Emptiness!" "Bereftness!" "Say *what*?"
"As I always say,
 Idleness is the nigger in the Devil's woodpile."
"Jus' goes to show ya
Money don't buy a guy happiness."
"Yeh, he'd become despondent." "And no children,
No close family to fill in the gaps
Don't help none neither." "He'd grew despondent,
Who, by all rights, shoulda been on Easy Street."
"Boys, let me jus' tell yous one thing!
I'm glad as hell to be right here, right now,
Chewin' the fat with you yahoos,
And ain't nobody gonna get me t'agree
To givin' up the goat that easy;
When I go, assumin' I ever decide to,
You can damn well bet
I'm goin' out breech, not headfirst,
Screamin' loud enough to wake the dead . . .
Even ol' Purvis, poor bastard!"

Moe in the Desert

At this spectral a.m. hour,
When the Square is as bare as a defoliated tree
And the horizon hasn't yet decided
What rags to pull from which clothes hangers
To wear on this new day's desert trek,

I silently materialize,
My wide eyes belying drowsiness
As I head to the Capital Café for breakfast.
My tentative steps traverse the broken sidewalk
From the *Bugle* office, where I've worked early

With Editor Wedemeyer, correcting typos,
Rewriting copy, and adding last-minute obituaries.
As I approach the Courthouse,
An ear-splitting noise explodes from shit-splattered ledges,
Niches, eaves, sills, and concrete steps:

A plague of dismal pigeons weighted with chaos
Swoops into the aghast sky
And, like a pterodactyl chasing slower prey,
Makes two complete gyrations around the building
Before roosting again in murmurous silence.

But the persistence of their hysterical flapping
Deafens me; in every direction,
The shapes I bring into focus change to wings,
Wings to pennons, thrashing like palm fronds,
Edging Swifty's Preowned Car Lot,

Pennons to rows of mercury-vapor shadows
Escaping choking throats of lampposts,
Throwing themselves at the mercy of the Courthouse,
Pleading *nolo contendere* to morning's suit,
The tattered, anachronistic 48-star flag

Slapping against its rust-flaked pole
Above a patinated, bronze-plaqued cenotaph,
Bedizened with plastic nosegays,
Commemorating the "Ultimate Sacrifice"
Made by a few dozen Lapinga County souls.

Entering the café, I'm suddenly accosted by squawking —
Buzzards huddling over their own fresh carrion.
I take my seat; they take no notice of me,
A latter-day Moses
Even this community's vultures won't eye, let alone eat.

Icarus in Lapinga

As I approach the Capital Café's glass doors
This unconscionably cold morning,
When the illuminated Time/Temp sign,
Angling out like a hitchhiker's thumb
From the Lapinga Savings and Loan,
Across the street at the four-way stop,
Reads 9 degrees at 7:57,
The rooster sun, lusting over this "bedroom community"
As though each Downtown building were a horny hen
It intends to mount and fertilize,
Flies into my eyes, flapping and scratching.

I enter the café, blinded momentarily,
Grope for my seat as though in a labyrinth.
An image of mythical Icarus soaring sunward,
His wax wings melting, comes to mind
As I plop into my window booth
And begin floating in a sea
Moiling with breaching, screeching Minotaurs,
Hoping to survive until once again
Trusty Imagination can save me
From the destructive element
Into which I've been wittingly sucked.

Slowly vision refocuses my location;
My senses are assaulted by the persiflage
Wafting above the back table like body odors,
Emanating from quasi-familiar faces
Behind the fiats, admonitions, epithets,
Regurgitated expletives, and denigrating platitudes
About "separate-but-equal" treatment for "niggers,"
Lesser yet for the "greedy Jew";
"Mongrelization!
That's what you've got in St. Louis!"
"Thank God we ain't got many of them bastards here!"

My eyes wince, and my ears cringe
As the conversation advances, retreats
From a rehearsed sermon on the White Man's Burden
To a listing of inferior physical characteristics,
Rising to raucous climax as Master of Ceremonies, Dubart,
Duly self-appointed Exalted Grand Dragon,
Demonstrates "thick lips" of "Hate i-ans" and "Zoo-loos"
He witnessed during his war days in the South Pacific
By squeezing both his bloated cheeks:
"They'd swing through the 'cokeynut' trees
Like brush apes and go-rillas — naked niggers."

Suddenly the coffee I've been swilling
To warm my belly turns acidic;
Now my thawing thoughts dissolve into reality,
And I realize how I've victimized my ego
Likening myself to Icarus.
Nonetheless, these Capital Café regulars,
With a stretch, just could be kings of Crete,
Each a vindictive Minos wanting to punish me
For being the son of some uppity-Hebe Daedalus,
Who just might encourage "nigras" and "kikes,"
Each named Theseus, to elope with their Ariadnes.

Messianic Vestiges

Once again, Lapinga's gentry
Have been exonerated, made the recipients
Of a mid-February reprieve from daily labors.

Last night's blizzard, their stay of execution,
Is in glistening evidence even at 8 a.m.
On the plate glass of the Capital Café,

Through whose smoke-smudged, rippled windows
Regulars glimpse the prismatical day,
Measure its potential intensity

In shadows lifting like venetian blinds
Raised by invisible hands
On the facades of stores not yet open

And against the monolithic Courthouse,
Whose anomalous Greek face
Wears a look of quizzical amazement.

One by one, prerecorded voices enter
And seek their own levels at sections of the back table,
Divided according to hierarchies.

At one end are seated Deputy Sheriff "Butch" Wampler,
Episcopalian Reverend Snavely,
High-school agribusiness teacher Chester Heck,

Who doubles as Driver's Ed instructor
To supplement his meager self-image and income,
And Supers Oder and Birdsong of the city's two utilities;

Each is a Whitman's Sampler or Da Vincian genius
On local, state, and federal politics,
The most current quotes

On June and August corn and beans,
Hogs and barrows on and off the hoof,
Recent robberies, accidents, probates, drug busts,

God's latest manifestations of Grace and disgrace,
The cost of power bought for resale
To their economically anorexic small town.

Two chairs down, Buster Godwin,
Owner of the local roller rink,
Argues with the Chevy-Buick dealer, Clement Farquar,

Over the deregulation of fuel prices
And public transportation
As though both had a vested interest in lobbying

Or were privy to "inside" information
By which they might influence the nation's future.
A third, City Manager Mort Fudd,

Considers his silence a valuable contribution
To the discussion; he times his nods
To coincide like applause with each brief pause

While these friendly opponents
Unleash Demosthenes-chat from their slingshots
Without taking time to aim.

A stone's throw away, where two adjacent tables
Have been permanently coupled
Like dogs stuck after copulation,

A quorum of the City's Aldermen convenes;
Their lofty civic demeanors,
The rhetoric that issues forth with gravity,

And the whisperous surreptitiousness
Of their occasional collective huddles
Elevate them to a state of transcendence,

Endow them, somehow,
With a vague yet plausibly austere resemblance
To the supping Disciples;

Depending on through whose eyes they're viewed,
They all bear a likeness to Christ
Or Judas, the mendacious one.

Regardless of the perspective taken by their audience,
They represent the spiritual antithesis;
No in-between roles exist

For these devoted servants to assume:
Martyrdom hovers above them sublimely
Like the ethereal halo of their cigarette smoke.

This café, an embodiment of its former soul,
Becomes a cathedral, almost Gothic,
A breathing reincarnation

Echoing with Christian guffaws,
Messianic laughter, charismatic catcalls and hilarity
Amidst intermittent pseudo/sado-seriousness.

Suddenly, and with mystical prestidigitation,
Owner Fred Grabhorn, robed in priestly surplice —
An apron stained with egg yolks and grease —

Throws open the front doors to let morning's vapors
Flow through the hallowed portal;
Crystal, frigid air, like divine inspiration,

Rushes in, labors to insinuate itself
Into whatever bronchioles of the room's lungs
Might still be unviolated by human pollution;

The infusion is slow to occur.
Even more metaphysical is the transfiguration
That begins to purge this inner sphere,

Clear away diaphanous tobacco haze,
And permit light to resuscitate the dimness.
One by one, the regulars pay,

Most three thin dimes for two-hour coffee,
Then leave to make token show
Of opening their own doors for a snowbound town.

Empty at last by half past ten, the eatery lapses;
Those who run this glorified soup kitchen,
Chef Fred, head waitress Sue and her retinue,

With less than an hour to prepare for extended lunch,
Take five; those who've disappeared
Behind cloistered counters, desks, and cash registers

Hastily knot loose ends so as to be ready by noon
To resume more sacerdotal matters
Back at the Capital Café in Lapinga's Gethsemane.

Moe's Package Vacation

"Gone and back! Gone and back!"
The Capital Café's fair-skinned waitress
Remarks on my absence, celebrates my return
With steaming coffee and a smile.

For a week, my wife and I "vacationed" in Jamaica,
Stayed in a sleazy Ocho Rios hotel
Decorated in well-worn American-50s-motel motif,
Boasting a fake white sand beach on the Caribbean Sea.

All week, we ate our "three squares" there
According to a regimentally set schedule (a half-hour each)
In a prisonlike environment presided over
By ill-trained natives dressed in vestigially colonial uniforms,

Waiting on impatient international tourists
(Captives to their nontransferable meal plans),
Carrying Blue Mountain brew in one hand,
Cream in the other, placing too many spoons sideways

On the fly-infested tabletops,
Supplying more glasses and varisized plates
Than we'd ever use to portion out juices,
Croissants, mangoes, star apples, gooseberries.

Now, squirming over the booth's tape-mended leatherette,
Staring down at the viscid remains
Of gravy biscuits and fried eggs on a chipped plate,
Then out through the rippled windows

Fronting Liberty Street and the Courthouse,
Focusing on this typically mid-Missouri,
End-of-March snowfall
Trapping crocus, tulips, forsythia in freeze frame,

I know in my heart my spirit has returned to Lapinga;
Rain forest and sunshine jumped ship
Somewhere in the West Indies,
Left me to tack back in crude winds

Devoid of fragrant spices, hibiscus scents,
And heated-breeze-screeching ferns and palm trees.
Yet ironically, being home again,
Marooned on this "lily-white" island, is a relief.

The Passing of Chet Jekyll

With more frequency than ever before,
He's located his spirit soaring off course,
A blip on his mind's radarscope
Slowly fading out of range, into obscurity.

And whenever he's entered Memory's storeroom
To take inventory of existing stock,
Double-check his tabulations,
He's been unable to account for entire categories.

Daily this condition plagues him
In strange and quirky ways:
He addresses old acquaintances with names
Appropriated from cop dramas and soap operas,

Forgets which day of the week it is,
In which year of which decade
He chose to deposit his monthly disability
And Social Security checks.

This Friday morning,
Loitering in the Capital Café,
Not listening to the claptrap of regulars,
Sipping from a trick coffee cup

That seems to refill itself continuously
From a hidden artesian well,
He suddenly realizes amnesia commands his senses:
Table, chair, light fixture, fan

Stare back at him like a family of deer
Frozen near road's edge by probing headlights;
He can't see them in the bleak darkness
That has eclipsed his static synapses.

His collapsing psychic apparatus
Has rendered him deaf and dumb, numb;
His entire body is a foot that's fallen asleep.
Deep breaths only increase disorientation

As faces, shapes lose depth of field,
Suck him into their swirling vortex:
He shivers, chokes in a final stroke-throe,
Slumps in his seat, unnoticed for almost an hour.

Emancipation Proclamation

This soft May a.m.
Is riffled and shimmering with rain-glaze,
Silent as amniotic caves.
Only occasional cars,
Weaving the Square's four slick streets
Into a bracelet of glistening strands,
Break the tranquility with their sibilant swishing.

Through the Capital Café's open double doors
Pours a thick, foreboding smoke-haze
Billowing from the back table
Like a scrim net descending or tidal wave
Ripsawing shoreward in a gray, swirling nimbus
That emanates from eight saintly faces
Engaged in alternately responsive conversations.

My disciplined senses of wisdom and equanimity,
Which usually hold fixed positions against the enemy,
Desperately quiver listening to Homer LaChance,
Retired Chief Loan Officer of Lapinga S&L,
Debate inflation's Medusa-like manifestations
With Gentry Gander, MFA claims adjuster,
And Casey Laidlaw, sales agent for Pugg Realty,

While Ned Oder and Festus Birdsong,
Supervisors of the City Light and Water companies,
Respectively, keep the faith,
Refrain from cross-pollinating the symposium.
By degrees, compounded of ignorance and indifference,
The subject shifts, as it inevitably must,
To sports, divorces, necrologies, foreclosures, felonies,

And profane bigotries aimed at "niggers" and "Jews,"
In no particularly predictable order.
Although normally the overly loquacious Deacon,
Keith Priestly, of the Third Baptist Church,
Has the first and terminal words
Between whose questionably collective parentheses
The rest assert their views edgewise,

This heated morning, druggist Otto Scruggs,
Barber Mel Dubart, grocer Elmer Snell,
And Chevy-Buick dealer Clement Farquar
Silence the garrulous Deacon with their sardonic remarks
Regarding the "nigger" State Highway Patrol officer
Who moved into town, on South Maple, last week
To set up an outpost in Lapinga County.

Swigging coffee dregs, gathering my effects,
I pay, race from the café south down Liberty,
Past spirea bordering the Courthouse lawn,
Slip almost unnoticed into the *Bugle* office,
And settle at my desk to begin the arduous editing.
But scanning the top sheet of numerous proofs,
I cringe at the lead story's banner headline:

**LAPINGA GETS STATES' FIRST
NEEGRO HIWAY PATROL MAN!!!**

"Lions Meet Here"

It's not even 7:15,
Yet the mid-Missouri heat
Is gathering just beneath the macadam
To mount an offensive against sensibilities
Already debilitated by birthright and franchise.
Scions of scions of lead miners,
Farm hands, day laborers, merchants, professionals,
And state-hospital patients leashed to their drugs
Hover just above the town
Like buzzards bearing an eerie resemblance to wraiths.

Behind the closed doors of this café,
Where I, "Perfesser Fischer" to most, come to breakfast
And gather courage through stimulation
From the sacred brown elixir
To mount my own assault on the great enemy, Humidity,
A rented film is playing
To a packed, leonine audience
Intent on cementing their sense of patriotic duties;
Periodically, cheers and shouts rise
As they applaud a triumphant Popeye or Mighty Mouse,

Then lapse back into mesmerized silence
While lumps of gravy biscuits,
Hash browns, sausage links, ham, and toast
Leap from lip-cliffs in nutritional suicide
And dive into double- and triple-chin abysses.
When I look up from my newspaper,
Their rapacious faces are filing past me
Like war machines crossing a desert
To rendezvous with creatures of certain defeat;
My eyes recognize their sanctimonious features

Neither as those of ghosts, poets, dreamers,
Nor as dandelion spores floating in the imagination;
Not attorneys nor morticians
Dressed in factory-outlet-reject three-piece suits
Or mismatched, double-knit leisure slacks and jackets;
*

Not First Freewill Baptist preachers and elders
Robed in holier-than-thou rhetoric;
Not prize-bull toilers of the earth, shopkeepers,
Bankers with disdain for investors from the City
But babies seraphic, roseate, naked.

Each recognizes me as the retired schoolteacher;
As they leave the café,
Their perfunctory waves, winks, and nods
Barely acknowledge my negligible presence.
Despite living in this community for more than a decade,
I doubt any of them even know my "Christian" name.
Anyway, I realize why I'm here:
To record the release of the Lions Club from their cage
And their invasion of Downtown's coliseum,
Where fellow Christians wait to be eaten alive.

Dog Daze and Loony Cats

Each 6 a.m., six days a week,
These hounds sever familial intimacies,
Desert sleeping bitches, twitching litters.
Some come to breakfast
Directly from last evening's mistresses,
Those wanton strangers
Whom others of their brotherhood leave by 1 a.m.
In Lapinga Hotel cages
Before first returning home to their neutered solitudes,
While yet others of the pack abandon dreams
To gather at the Capital Café;
They're all phantasms dogging their own shadows,
Each a misbegotten vapor sifting out of night
Into glazed twilight like topiary fog
In the shapes of canine creatures:

Humane Society mongrels, mutts, curs,
Street breeds, hybrids, Heinz 57s,
Even a few best-in-show, blue-ribbon winners
Howling to be let out of Drowsing's kennel,
Admitted into palatial courtyards
Where their fully awakened imaginations
Might cavort with Louie XIV's castoff whores,
Babbitt's sensual, if elusive, fairy-child,
Or Rosie the Riveters waiting at castle gate,
The Capital Café's front doors,
Like its overly solicitous waitresses —
These regulars lifting their verbal legs,
Sullying, yellowing, causing to wilt and die
Every formal garden held sacred
In Lapinga's hundred-and-fifty-year history.

Except for Sundays, they run their territories,
Compelled and as utterly orderly as astral rotations,
Then converge on their tenaciously held fellowship
Of community watchdogs
To bark derisions and obscenities
At winos, junkies, rapists, and mental cases
*

Released on their own Thorazined recognizance,
Outpatient crazies all,
Who daily cross their hallucinatory London Bridge
Connecting State Hospital #8
With the Lapinga Courthouse Square,
Where they malinger just outside the Capital Café doors —
The town's alley cats, held at bay,
Mewing halfheartedly
At morning's faintly visible polestar and Lorelei moon.

The Visigoth

The size of a pregnant sow
Having just emerged from wallowing in a mudhole,
He throws open both glass doors:
The Capital Café's Red Sea parts.
His Alaric-vastness asserts itself
As, on porcine legs and trotters,
He forges toward the green marble counter
And, like a pig waddling to a trough,
Negotiates between tightly spaced tables,
Then balances his amorphous enormity on the stool.
His massive ass overlaps its circumference
Like baking cupcakes oozing out of their wrappers;
Blue Big Smith bibs,
Resembling a pork-sausage casing
Straining to contain human stuffings,
Balloon, threaten to explode,
Spew their contents with one more movement.
His dirty shirt, a truce flag
Meant to spare stray eyes cruel and unusual abuse,
Can't cover his portly-boar belly,
Which in another environ might easily be mistaken
For that of an obese rhino, hippo, tapir,
Or grotesque dinosaur roaming the nether regions.
His adjustable, green seed cap,
Pointing backwards over his coarse hair,
Fails to shade a face and snout so corpulent
All features seem to swirl toward a common vortex,
His swinish mouth, and smudge —
God's thumbprint pressed into a red ink-pad
Bleeding within his blond beard's bristly halo.

This heroic figure, new to our community,
Who may stay a month or so
Before assuming his next assignment,
Heads the Safeway Wrecking Co.'s crew,
Hired by County Court order
To dismantle the old Lapinga Hotel,
Condemned last month for the fifth and final time
*

After a rain-laden back wall
Collapsed onto C Street.
For now, those who rule the "deacon's seat"
Remain subservient to his eminence.
After all, each day
He carts away amidst the bricks, rafters,
Plaster dust, reusable doors, sashes,
Two-by-fours, three-by-twelves,
Stained-glass windows, and transom units,
Not to mention potentially salable toilets and tubs,
At least eighty years of their heritage.
These days, it's not always so easy
To watch history disintegrate into thin air,
Even for these elite guild members of Lapinga,
Knowing they have no adequate replacement
For their town's collective memory.
Reluctantly they allow him to grunt, squeal,
Hold court, seize center stage,
Realizing that in a few more weeks,
Even if their Square will be one fortress less,
Progress three steps closer to the Past,
At least they'll have regained complete control
Over the sacking of their own Carcassonne.

Lost in the Wilderness

Purposefully, I awaken earlier than daybreak,
Cast off from my sand-land sleep,
In which fantasies of reaching Canaan
Incubate in heated quiescence.
I rise from lying beside my dutiful wife
And peer through translucent pupils
As if hoping to spy a burning bush,
Ram caught in a thicket,
Or gushing rock by an oasis
That might signal my imminent approach to
Or arrival in the Promised Land —
Any sign to let me intuit divine design.

Back to reality, I bathe and groom, dress,
Manage to locate the appropriate key
To set my car's dependable engine in motion,
Then enter the 80-degree darkness.
I twice traverse Freedom and Liberty streets,
As if looking for yesterday's faces,
Before parking my Chevrolet
In the alley behind the Capital Café,
Where I'll have breakfast
Prior to heading for the *Lapinga Bugle* office
To proofread for Thursday's paper
Or help Editor Wedemeyer revise his column.

Once positioned in my usual booth,
I listen with vulpine acuity
To the regulars' garrulity:
City burghers, arbiters of public mores and taste,
And armchair political advisors
Heatedly deciding civil-rights issues
Recently surfaced through the news media's cesspool,
Setting adrift derisive pieties, sacrilegious epithets
Relating to Mississippi's "freedom riders."
I visibly wince each time the group,
Hooded collectively
In its cigarette smoke's opaque cloak,

Tells a gratuitous "country witticism/Jew-joke"
Or decries "niggers," "jigaboos," "jungle bunnies,"
Hurling their entire "e-boney crew"
Into the recently excavated abyss
Of Forsyth County's hissing racist activists:
"At least somebody out there
Still's got the guts to speak their 'peace,'
Call a spade a spade,
Put them lazy black bastards back in their place."
Suddenly barber Dubart, unable to contain himself, erupts,
"What's black and white and got two good eyes?
Sammy Davis, Jr., and 'Mushey' Dayan!"

And I can't help wondering why they've spared me.
Legend has it that back in the '30s and '40s,
Lapinga's civic-minded leaders
Lynched, castrated, and set all the rest
Of "them nigra yahoos runnin' overnight express
To save their black asses."
As for Jews, I can only speculate
That perhaps we've always been too few
To pose a threat to this "Five-Star" community
Or that they've missed us looking for beasts with two heads,
Red eyes, buzzard's beak, and three green tails.
Regardless, I know I'll never reach Canaan alive.

Last Day in the Old Capital Café

Outpatients, realtors, insurance and car salesmen,
Deputy Sheriff, C.P.A., veterinarian,
Civil servants, bankers, merchants, attorneys,
Even a retired high-school English teacher,
A Jew to boot, from St. Louis,
Congregate for the last time
Inside these sacrosanct temple walls.
Sue seems unusually distracted, even a bit gloomy,
As if, after fifteen years in the same maze,
Change, no matter how potentially convenience-laden,
Just can't replace habit, routine,
And certainly not her spinster stepsisters,
Her co-waitresses, who've already proclaimed
They won't be moving uptown
With chef Fred and his crew,
Really only five doors up and over on C Street,
In the prefab that's sprouted like a weed
On the lot of the recently razed Lapinga Hotel.

By Monday, the Capital Café
Will face the Courthouse from the north, not east,
Occupying a classier piece of real estate.
Whether it will still attract its steady clientele
Isn't really the issue,
Though they've made it preeminently so
These past three weeks.
Just now, each of the boys
Debates the advent of tomorrow's auspicious a.m.
As though he personally has a stake in it:
Will they come aboard or jump ship
For Slick's Quick Shop, out at highway's edge?
All are secretly "pleased as piss"
That chef Fred and his staff
Obviously lack just enough business acumen to quit.
He should have realized long ago
That you can't squeeze blood
Out of two fried eggs and a rasher of bacon
Or stacks of flapjacks with five sausage patties
*

(Either for $1.59,
Including bottomless cups of coffee,
Flowing as if from aquifers,
Thrown in for good measure)
Without being funded by the federal government
Or nefarious activities
Conducted after hours out the back door.

Nonetheless,
They work the subject for all it's worth,
Chew all its nutrients;
Then, as the clock hands advance toward 9,
Each pledges his vote of confidence:
Loyal, steadfast, faithful as the day is long,
Appreciative-as-hell, well-wishing regulars,
They'll be there at the crack of morrow's dawn
To help celebrate the ribbon-cutting ceremony
Along with Mayor Mel Dubart and Chamber Prexy Pugg
By partaking of a Barmecide feast
Of "*Dognuts* + *Java* . . . All You Can Eat . . . *Gradus* . . .
On The House . . . *No Charge* . . . **FREE**."

LAPUTA, MO.

Pop. (est.) 2119

Along toward ten oclock I went up front. There was a drummer there. . . . We got to talking about crops.

"There's nothing to it," I says, "Cotton is a speculator's crop. They fill the farmer full of hot air and get him to raise a big crop for them to whipsaw on the market, to trim the suckers with. Do you think the farmer gets anything out of it except a red neck and a hump in his back? You think the man that sweats to put it into the ground gets a red cent more than a bare living," I says. "Let him make a big crop and it wont be worth picking; let him make a small crop and he wont have enough to gin. And for what? so a bunch of damn eastern jews I'm not talking about men of the jewish religion," I says, "I've known some jews that were fine citizens. You might be one yourself," I says.

— from *The Sound and the Fury*, William Faulkner

"Oh, yes, this is a wonderful govment, wonderful. Why, looky here. There was a free nigger there, from Ohio; a mulatter, most as white as a white man. . . . They said he could *vote*, when he was at home. Well, that let me out. Thinks I, what is the country a-coming to?"

— from *The Adventures of Huckleberry Finn*, Mark Twain

Out of the Cradle, Endlessly Grousing

Conversation in Laputa's stifling Capital Café
Sounds more like the screeching of ibises
Than the facetious grousing
Among easygoing townspeople and farmers.

Pronouncements about "not-up-to-snuff" cows and sows
Preempt the 7 a.m. news
Squeaking through an antique Philco radio;
Profundities surrounding the specter of drought

And the need for anima and a touch of luck
To raise corn, beans, sorghum, and wheat this season
Emanate from these Ptolemaic sages
Convened to bribe the Meteorological Gods of the Grain.

The cradle of Midwestern civilization
Resides right here between State Highway AA
And the Lake of the Ozarks, 50 miles south.
Nearby, Osiris, in bib overalls, slouches.

Arcady in Laputa

Poets, politicians, philosophers:
Farmers, factory hands, vendors, vets, repairmen,
Grease monkeys, bankers, brokers —
Sodbuster sages all —
Deliberate, gesticulate, expectorate,
Then deteriorate into high rhetoric,
Base reason, and mediocre, if emphatic, bullshit;
Insignia sewn onto their seed caps,
Like tattered pennons flying from rickety poles
Of shepherds' mountainside tents,
Advertise their identities on the acrid air.

Only these Laputian Demostheneses,
These Midwestern a.m. Aristotles and Platos,
5 o'clock Socrateses, Dracos,
Alexanders the Great and Average,
And other celebrities of the Golden Age of Redneckery
Remain ethically pristine, adamant and tenacious
In their opposition to the new humanism
That preaches equality of birthright
And tolerates freedom of speech and worship
For niggers, hippies, commies, queers, and kikes
As requisites for society's survival.

They've prevailed, despite the winds of change
Slandering inland from Montgomery and Selma,
Haight-Ashbury and Greenwich Village,
By refuting the ubiquitous enemies of "Truth":
TV and the newspapers.
Each abides by his deep-seated belief
That the first city is celebrated yet
As the Confederacy's original capital,
The second as the home of Yazoo Brush Hogs,
And that the latter two districts
Are iniquitous dens of radical, satanic depravity.

Not once have they deviated from professing,
Through unadorned bigotry, prejudice,
Calumniation, crude black humor, outright hatred,
*

Scurrilous xenophobia toward all interlopers,
And expletives studiously selected
To gain the most putrescent public effect,
Their collective allegiance to the supremacy
Of an unadulterated white race, predominantly Baptist;
Self-elected, die-hard defenders of Democracy,
These vigilantes stand united and ready, semper fi-ed,
To combat all threats to their American way of life.

Although the Capital Café, a converted gas station
Located at Laputa's crossroads,
Is an unlikely veil of Arcady,
It's convenient to every hayseed
In this pastoral Athenian community.
In blind retreat they come each morning;
Enlightened, they leave after three hours' discourse
On laying pipe, feeding livestock,
Cursing the weather, contemplating next season's planting,
Pursuing life, liberty, their own happiness,
And pay homage to the gods that be.

A Cradle of Civilization

Twelve Pharaohs,
Seated at three hastily joined tables,
Compete to be heard:
Sinecures are being awarded by patronage,
And laws distorted to meet their most self-serving needs.
Actually, from the very beginning,
Rectitude and piety were their sole guides,
Provided they never applied to royalty.
In times of plenty, felonies and misdemeanors
Were treated with the same degree of rapacity
Employed in the sacking of enemy city-states.
But in flood time,
When people below the Golden City
Were wont to steal from need rather than greed,
Their leniency would commute hundred-year sentences
To ten tilling date and fig groves.
And in times of plague and drought,
Even doubting Pharaohs placed their hopes in the afterlife.

As in ancient days,
When leaders commemorated themselves publicly
With monuments such as this, the Capital Café,
Where, each morning, from 5 to 10,
These latter-day Pharaohs gather in consultation
To determine a nation's division of labor,
Slaves are still needed to maintain the status quo.
But these days, with so much peace to accommodate,
They find it difficult
To exact servitude from work crews,
Especially when summer bakes the grain in its fields.
They agree their vassals lack spirit;
Lethargy and malingering are epidemics
Brought on by Ethiops and the people of Moses.
This week, they'll fabricate convenient edicts
Banishing them from this Nile-like land,
Doom them, as they did their ancestors,
To the Two Lost Tribes of Niggers and Kikes.

Capital Café Clock

The all-seeing advertising clock,
Rimmed in blue neon,
Flips a hundred painted cards every hour.
Reading their Day-Glo slogans,
He watches fifty pass
Like knights charging into battle.

Nothing here breaks expectation;
The names reappear every five minutes
With unfamiliar sameness: car parts, clothing,
Furniture, tractors and trucks, the one barbershop,
Sears, ready-mix, propane, appliances, wedding gowns —
Prepackaged America at "wholesale" prices.

At a nearby table, twelve squires,
Whose heraldry rides astride the lighted dial
Above the cluttered front counter,
Preside over each a.m. in shining armor,
Contriving fire sales and loss-leader promotions
To renew their fealty to Queen Greed.

He, Nate Rosenbloom,
Developer of the Factory Outlet Mall
At the Lake of the Ozarks, an hour from here,
Is a stranger to this round-table conclave.
They have no idea that his mission,
A Grail quest of sorts,

Will eventually force them out of business.
Although the plug's in its socket,
The clock's hands have quit (God knows how long ago!);
He doubts any of them has ever stopped to notice
It's always 3 o'clock in this crossroads Camelot
Or that he, disguised in suit and tie, is Merlin the Magician.

Helen Among the 12 Disciples

Chair legs claw the Capital Café's concrete floor
With raw, bawdy screeches
As the men in seed caps take their seats
This autumn-cool June morning.
The blond, eighteen-year-old, rouge-cheeked waitress
With blue-mascaraed eyelashes,
Wearing faded Levi's
And a gauzy blouse over breasts with erect nipples,
Arouses their drowsy minds,
Brings blood rushing through plaque-clogged arteries
From throbbing hearts to flaccid private parts.

Like hands groping in the dark,
A babel of unredeemed voices
Reaches to grab her alabaster arms.
Dressed, she stands naked before them, unabashed,
Waiting for them to discover a common mother tongue
With which to order eggs, ham steaks, hash browns,
Gravy biscuits, Texas toast,
Bottomless cups of industrial-drip coffee,
And three platters of fresh, fatty gossip;
As her bouncing body floats away,
They turn momentarily stony.

She arrives before 5 each dawn
To be violated by viperine tongues and lupine eyes
Used to guiding buyers to shelves and bins,
Sows and cows to troughs;
But their coat-and-tie, bib-overalled protocol
Fails to reduce her silky silence
To snide asides and mordant retorts,
Though she's been known to sting them with a reprisal.
Just now, she returns from the kitchen,
Flits amidst them like a bee,
Pollinating their base desires with her smile.

A heifer in heat, she crazies them,
Breathing impotent desire down their spines.
Her few words render each subservient
As though she were Isis, Goddess of Fertility,
Ruling a region of semi-civilized Egyptians
Thirsting in the desert for their first wet dream.
With prurient intent, all succumb to her beauty.
They would worship her pagan form
Were she not Reverend Bone's eldest daughter, Helen,
The town's notorious whore,
A harlot among disciples of the Lord.

Under Laputa: Poet, Pass By

The parking lot is a potluck supper
Whose salmagundi consists of tourist vans,
Horse trailers, campers, delivery trucks,
A solitary semi with its engine snoring,
Three decked-out Harleys,
And the local armada of pickups.

Although he's not passed through here in nearly a year,
Everything seems just as he left it,
A time capsule containing memorabilia
Of Laputa's Capital Café,
A Walker Evans documentary photo,
An arrested mixed metaphor:

From indigenous Virgils, Homers, Juvenals,
And myriad Cincinnati
Gathering for repast, sharing social repose
And moral succor from each other's brotherhood
Over biscuits and red-eye gravy,
Smoked ham steaks, Texas toast, and molten coffee,

Speculating, debating, pontificating
On blighted milo, stunted soybeans, sickly chickens,
And the shameful prices of slaughter hogs and beef,
To the teenage waitress, Ellen,
Or Nell, Helen, or Suella Somebody,
Disporting her seductive butt in skimpy jeans

And perfectly juggled, lodestone-like breasts
Beneath a see-through blouse,
Which magnetize the men's eyes like iron filings;
From the nondimensional, four-by-sixteen mural
Depicting sky, sea, palm tree, and unseen beach at sunset,
To the neon-rimmed advertising clock,

Not a single item has shifted position
Nor any regular player quit the stage,
Changed roles in this daily psychodramatic soap opera —
With one obvious exception, that is!
He no longer finds himself amused, affected, provoked,
Motivated to compose a sonnet or ode

To this mythically proportioned Capital Café,
With its Christian, Greco-Roman, and Egyptian protagonists.
Perhaps time has dulled his vision,
Which transfigures Reality's turnips and sows' ears
Into blood of the Lamb and silk purses.
Sadly, this place is now just the gas station

Where he, Clayton Ladue, used to fill up
On trips through Missouri and other remote nations,
Not a place to stimulate his alchemic imagination.
Whatever the case may be,
He laments his inability to transmute Truth
And lose himself in a hallucinatory fugue

Long enough to create from nothing something
Before driving on to give a poetry reading
At the university in Columbia tonight.
Maybe someday the Muse will inspire him again
To write about this thousand-and-first Laputa
He's passed by on his magic-carpet rides.

Round Table Café

Green, red, and blue seed caps,
Baggy pants, work shirts, mud-caked boots,
Calloused hands, and furrowed facial landscapes
Eroded by sixty seasons
Of alternating blazing summers in fields
With freezing winters indoors
Accompany speech with a spicy dialect
Salted and peppered with pungent expletives
Slowly cold-rolled like steel through fire.
Seed caps, green, red, and blue,
Emblazoned with labels — sewn coats of arms —
Display dominions, orders, degrees:
Funk's G-Hybrid, Phister, Pioneer —
The heraldry of an ancient granger community.

Green-billed, red-meshed, and blue-ribbed,
The hats could easily be perceived as pennants
Fluttering above striped tents
Where a medieval tournament is being held
To decide chivalry and highest valor
In to-the-death duels.
Here honors are bestowed
On the basis of loudness in jousting,
Tedium in broadsword thrust and parry,
Vulgarity in the art of repartee,
Claptrap with forked-tongue pike,
And balderdash and blather with spiked ball and chain,
Victor and vanquished alike
Pardoned for their fanciful flights from reason.

Whether Christians whispering rumors of Jesus,
Wishing to go to the Holy Land in quest of the Grail,
Knights riding in search of distressed Maid Marians
To save from disgraceful, barbaric rapaciousness,
Or just capitalistic agribusinessmen
Meeting for 5-to-10 o'clock breakfast at the Capital Café
Before advancing on 100-degree heat,
Hog troughs, commodities, or retirement,
*

They converge beneath their plumed, visored helmets —
Ubiquitous seed caps —
These avaricious Friar Tucks, Little Johns, and Robin Hoods
Of Laputa's Sherwood Forest,
Waiting, poised, to steal from the poor
And give back to the rich.

The Isle of Lesbos

The air inside the Capital Café
Is rife with hog-trough badinage,
Cash-register blather, and service-sector gripes.
Just now, debates progress
On the life expectancy of private enterprise
In light of higher taxes, on livestock inoculations,
The probability of drought and blight
Repeating last year's double-edged debacle,

And on the inscrutable circumstances
Surrounding "Red" Brewster's recent death.
Few accept the coroner's conclusion: natural causes.
Speculation runs high in favor of suicide
Catalyzed by his wife's estrangement,
Her abrupt flight
To take up residence in Vegas
With a flashy man of vague credentials.

Some hazard an uneducated guess
That stress from paying off notes on machinery
Purchased to make 1,000 acres produce
May have contributed to the tragedy;
Others scoff at the basically weak son-of-a-bitch
They always assumed "Red" to be
Beneath layers of humble dignity
And genuine Baptist piety.

Soon the eulogy for Brewster concludes,
But every head, instead of bowing,
Turns with burning curiosity
To assay two tourists,
Presumably on their way to the Lake of the Ozarks,
Who pass their table oblivious of them.
All eyes are slot-machine reels
Lining up on wild cherries

As one after another, spewing his jackpot,
Recognizes the bleached blonde in hot pants
As ill-fated "Red" Brewster's widow.
Although unable to place her companion,
They observe with growing outrage
Both nonchalantly holding hands,
Adoringly absorbed in their own brazen gazes,
Unafraid to be seen in Laputa's most public place.

In a moment of utter shock, vexation, and disgust,
Each self-elected arbiter of Laputian values,
Every vigilante empowered to safeguard his community,
This lush Arcady, with fervor and impunity,
Awakens to something never discussed:
The stuff of medieval plagues,
Witch hunts, inquisitions, autos-da-fé,
Poltergeists, chimeras, succubi, incubi, phantoms,

And real ghosts invading neighbors' houses,
Disrupting the essence of connubial bliss,
The steadfast relationship between man and wife,
The very bedrock of Judeo-Christian ethics,
Nature's mandate to copulate with the proper gender.
Gradually, their numb, knotted tongues,
Unaccustomed to being upstaged,
Nervously flicker back into laughterless claptrap.

But hours earlier than they would normally disperse,
The men flee by squeamish degrees,
And, as if forced to pay homage,
Each must pass Satan's table,
Where both women perpetuate their intimacies unabashedly,
Whispering Lesbian obscenities,
Kissing each other's lips passionately —
Desecrations these decent men will decry for weeks.

Hirsute

This morning, the Capital Café
Contains a quorum of quarreling orators.
Twenty filibusters are in progress simultaneously;
Only by exceeding supraliminal thresholds
Does one vested interest recognize another.

Then, with a single disparity — facial hair —
Laputa's Congressmen, senior and freshman alike,
Strike an uncommonly common chord of agreement:
They've convened to monitor the town's social mores
And reaffirm its supremacy over nearby Goshen.

Like their elders, the newly elected members
Drill wells, run farms, operate feedlots,
Set concrete driveways and sidewalks,
Dry-wall houses, repair telephone lines,
And raise hell with their 5-speed, 4-wheel-drive pickups.

The only way to tell them apart
From fellow statesmen in the prolonged final stages
Of chronic heartland disease,
Who caucus to vote each morning into being,
Is by their deviation from a clean-shaven face

And a close-cropped barbershop haircut.
Reluctantly, the incumbents accept their appearance
As the price paid for progress:
Wide sideburns resembling a mule's blinders
Protect their ears from direct frontal assaults;

Scraggly mustaches support red, veined noses;
Scruffy beards, like golf-course rough,
Landscape the fairways of their pocked, pink cheeks;
Under blue or green seed caps,
Human ccrn, sorghum, and wheat flourish to bumper crop.

Despite feigned public disapprobation,
The older men welcome the young generation into the fold,
Knowing that established hypocrisies
Will be maintained and time-honored bigotries exhumed
From the graves of their daily debates.

And as if to allay doubts about their qualifications,
They've fastened on an image from the Bible:
"If Christ could go around half-naked
And wear hair down to his ass,
These young brush apes can't be *all* that bad!"

Merchant Sailor

The itinerant Holsum Bread man
Keeps a pen behind his ear,
Sports a cropped mustache under his nose,
Wears white socks and black, lace-up utility shoes.

He sits alone at the counter,
Gulping high-octane coffee between dockings,
And concentrates on making an account entry
For his Capital Café delivery

In a dog-eared, leather-bound log
He keeps as would a fastidious ship captain,
Embracing it like a sacred scripture
When it's not buttoned in his back pocket.

Twice he extends a room's-length salutation,
His familiar echo and gestures
Reciprocating recognitions of his arrival
By farmers gathered to lament scorched corn

And by townspeople ambling in
To discuss "froze up" universal joints, twisted axles,
And snapped drive shafts
From last night's monster-truck and tractor pull.

He greets Helen, the teenage waitress of local breeding,
Who's stuffed into tight jeans
Accentuating her ample, pear-shaped buttocks;
Her smile is a sun at midnight

Among this lascivious contingent of "good old boys."
He winks furtively at her,
As though they've shared intimacies
Implausible in a community this size,

Then follows her languid swagger
Back to the fetid kitchen
As if his head were an anchor being raised
By capstan and winch to her deck

Instead of his brain-cage
Set aflame by visions of her naked breasts,
Plum-scented belly, and spacious delta
Swaying with amber waves of whole-grain wheat.

Something distracts his eyes,
Draws them to the open gold-cased pocket watch
He uses like a sextant to guide him
From harbor to slip in his Midwest Mediterranean.

He lays exact change on the counter,
Waits while Helen drops each coin in the register
And scribbles a receipt he requests,
On which she writes, "Twonite,"

Then leaves with a tumescent strut
Obvious to everyone but him.
Outside, he lingers just long enough
At the back of his laden truck

To rearrange its ballast of bakery goods —
Breads, buns, pies, cakes, doughnuts, muffins, and rolls —
He'll deliver along the trade route of his lust.
Before sealing the latch on the cargo hatch,

Casting off ropes, and setting sail,
He grabs fresh loaves of pumpernickel and sourdough,
Squeezes each in slow, profane delight,
Impatient to make Laputa's port again by high tide.

The Auction

Laputa's tight-fisted Grand Wizards of Wall Street
Confer early this Sunday morning
At the Capital Café
To interpret implications of yesterday's auction
Of Widow Scott's estate.
Jim Lapedes, the Chrysler-Plymouth dealer,
Leads the heated debate
Over devaluation of the dollar
And conspicuous consumption characterizing the sale.
He remarks, "You shoulda seed the prices
That damn junk pile of rugs brought,
Even if they was from 'Purrsia' and 'Brussel Sprouts,'
17th and 18th century."

Mortician Stiffmann intones, "I bid a hunderd-forty
On a backhoe too late; it went for one-thirty-five.
Later, they claimed me owner of a broke TV,
And I hadn't even bid."
The Scrogginses exclaim, "We seen sets of dishes
Bring six hunderd each
Just 'cause they had gold rims,
'Barbaria' and 'P-russia' printed on their backs."
"People'r sick," pontificates farmer Griesedieck.
"An inlaid dining-room 'suit' —
'Beauty-ful' equipment —
Went to some young kid I ain't never seed
For thirty-and-a-half hunderd beans."

"I'll tell you one thing," adds pharmacist Leech,
"We need to rethink our entire system!
When people can clip food coupons,
Draw stay-home pay through the week,
Then show up Saturday and drop a wad
On shit they wouldn' buy at the five-and-dime,
Somethin's wrong. What's the dif'rence
If it says 'Spow-dee,' 'Severs,' or 'Limogeez'
Instead of 'Nippon,' 'Korpa,' or 'Hong Prong'?
*

It's all made by foreign sons-of-bitches anyway!"
"All the power to them what's got it,"
Says Clootie the cop. "If I was black and sixty-five,
I'd have it made, too — in the spade . . . uh, shade!"

"Boys, I *gotta* get to church; it's late!"
Collective voices rise like grill smoke,
Gather, and break forth in common exhortation:
"Pray for us, Diamond Jim!"
The Chrysler-Plymouth dealer gazes sidelong,
His raised eyebrows shifty as snakes
Slithering away from danger.
He sneers, "Pray for yourselfs, boys.
It's gonna take all I got
Just to persuade God
To extend the loan He made me yesterday
So's I could buy one of them magic-carpet rugs
Eunice just *had* to have for our ratskeller."

The Origin of Species

At this 6 a.m. hour,
Aluminum cans and shattered beer bottles
Litter the Capital Café's gravel parking lot,
Ruled by pickup trucks, whose blunt front ends
Loom like thunderheads ready to explode,
And cars so old that travelers passing through
Could easily mistake this crossroads eatery
For a fully operational scrap yard.
As he approaches the front door,
These vehicles cast jagged shadows at his alien shape.
When he turns to look into their eyes,
Searing light from the rising sun,
Multiplied by twenty windshields,
Blurs his vision, makes him squint,
Blinds him to rifles mounted on racks,
CB antennas protruding conspicuously,
Outrigger side-view mirrors,
And bumpers covered with antediluvian mud.

Inside, tables and booths are Galápagos Islands
Floating in a concrete sea;
Each is populated with quasi-Caucasian natives
Speaking a strange, lazy patois.
Instead of Nate Rosenbloom,
Developer of the Factory Outlet Mall
At the Lake of the Ozarks,
He might be Darwin recording variations
In related, albeit exceedingly mutated, species:
Some have suits, others work boots and colorful caps
That wave like banners on the grease-soiled air,
Their insignia owing allegiance to "MFA,"
"Laputa Golf & Gun Club,"
"Joe & Ginger's Tropicana," "Red Man,"
"Funk's G-Hybrid," "John Deere," and "Pioneer Seeds."
Those wearing blue jeans and "Tuf-Nut" shirts
Socialize with lawyers and brokers in coats and ties,
Telephone- and gas-company servicemen in uniforms.

Similar in size, structure, and behavior,
They all appear to have inherited characteristics
Of identical prehistoric origin:
Faces equipped with beady, lupine eyes,
Mobile snouts, rubbery lips, spatulate tongues
That shape unintelligible sounds,
Prehensile hands that grasp greasy, rancid meats
And cups of lava-like java.
Each displays tropistic motions,
Sways from impulse to impulse, changing biases
According to pleasure and pain levels.
Like protozoa — paramecia, *Euglena*, and amebas —
They show no signs of abstract logic, reason, or insight.
This he realizes by the way they've begun encircling him
As he observes them from his booth.
Their savage stares are a fusillade of hurled spears.
Paying, fleeing, casting off his *Beagle*'s lines,
He barely escapes being eaten alive.

Vinnie Polenta Makes Two Service Calls

From his booth in the front window
Of the smoke-drenched Capital Café,
He envisions daring suitors
Scaling priveted courtyard walls
To rendezvous by night
With nubile Juliets and convent-bound Melibeas
Dressed to the neck in Lust's lacy disguise.

He sees a hundred Romeos, Calixtos,
And Tom Joneses tumbling half-naked
From loft windows, past iron grates
Covering basement openings
Just above castle moats,
Barely escaping with their dubious reputations intact,
Their raging libidos unscathed.

His rampant Fancy
Dances to the celebration of mating rites
Drifting across the ages,
Wafting about his ears on their way home
To be regenerated and electrified
By the shimmering dynamo
God fires to perpetuate the Life Force.

But when his eyes descend from the mist
Into which Imagination has strayed
While trying to prioritize this morning's schedule
Of computerized machines to service first at Judas Shoe,
To which he drives on a moment's notice from K.C.,
They distract the fleet teenager, Helen,
Petition her for the favor of her coffeepot,

And locate him amidst a gelded nobility
Of pretender princelings partaking of ribaldry,
Sedentary gossip, garrulity of a nature profane,
And calumniation, racially inspired,
Of all institutions, political, religious, and domestic:
An oligarchy glutted on cattle and poultry fatteners,
Satisfied with status quo impotency,

Infatuated by the notion of a Moral Majority
And Justice's ultimate obliteration
By patriotism and the Reaganized American Way
Of every bleeding-heart-liberal cause.
Suddenly a vague suspicion
That he's being stared at
Awakens him to the voluptuous waitress

Haloing his absent-mindedness,
Waiting for him to acknowledge her presence.
At such close range,
Her Botticellian body and face,
Visibly tumescent breasts with erect nipples,
Whisper his benign, cerebral blood alive;
His muted-lust blush invites her to pour;

Her smile bites him in the gonads;
He senses his flesh and bones being possessed
By the spirit of Don Juan Tenorio;
She creams his coffee with her lascivious motions
And musky aroma. Later this evening, at the Lorelei,
He knows he'll have her sewing machine
So well lubricated it'll be purring for all it's worth.

Running in Packs

He, Clayton Ladue, who works the Midwest,
Giving poetry readings at libraries, schools, and prisons,
Races from outdoors this frigid morning
Into the spastic blast of a gas space heater
And takes a seat out of its path
As though it might be a laser
About to cut his uncaffeinated brain in half.

Like an itinerant minister,
He occasionally makes Laputa's Capital Café his way station.
Inside, the radio is a coop of roosting hens;
A Seeburg Discotheque and cigarette dispenser
Are swaybacked horses asleep on their feet;
Vacant chairs, four to a table,
Are piglets cleaving to stolid sows' teats.

Like a child hiding from the world
Behind hands cupped over his eyes,
He squeezes his lids to pain,
But no transformations transport him;
The Here and Now refuses to dematerialize
Or let him imagine this shabby "grab-it-and-run"
As anything other than a converted filling station.

Through venetian blinds, he sees dawn's rays
Being steadily carpentered,
The sky nailed piece by tongue-and-groove piece
Into a partition dividing darkness from light
And painted with twilight's orange and purple hues.
Soon the spacious edifice will be complete,
Ready for occupancy by waking souls.

But the sharp-edged bark of a dog
Scratching at the café door shatters his image.
He overhears twelve of the regulars, most in bib overalls,
Seed caps, and boots, jeering lasciviously,
Their bellies rippling like waves
Emananting from a stone thrown into a stagnant pool
By a fool trying to imitate Creation.

At first he misses the connection the men make
Between mutt and waitress Helen Bone,
Who confesses the stray belongs to her.
They discern deeper, taller humor in her futility
As she shoos it from the entrance, sending it home.
Sodomy polka-dots their eyes and grins
With visions of her nude body

Strenuously mounted by the scraggly cur
They pruriently infer to be her secret lover.
As she sashays in and out of the kitchen,
They mix whispers with snickers and guffaws,
Sing the praises of leading a dog's life,
Testify to letting a sleeping dog "lay,"
"Rolling in the clover with Rover,"

And self-righteously remind themselves
Of the Biblical commandment
To keep an obstreperous pet locked in its cage
Or at least tied to its owner's bedpost,
Especially when it's of questionable pedigree.
Suddenly, the one they all call "Diamond Jim"
Breaks wind with a limerick worthy of Burns:

"Old Mother Hubbard went to the cupboard
To fetch her poor dog a bone,
But when she bent over, Rover took over
And gave her a bone of his own!"
The men collapse in a compost pile of laughter,
Heaped higher by Clootie the cop, who adds,
"Don't ya mean Old *Helen Bone* went to the cupboard?"

Decidedly uninspired by this doggerel recitation,
Ladue pushes aside plate and cup in disgust,
Pays the waitress whose namesake's face
Once launched a thousand Greek ships.
On leaving, he surveys these Laputians and sees instead
Twelve canines, paws on table, tails awag,
Howling insanely at the waning moon.

Moped

At this fog-enshrouded hour,
A baker's dozen-less-two of the boys
Congregate in the Capital Café to rehash the recent fire
That gutted Brown Bros. Furniture Store downtown.
They praise the uncharacteristic alacrity
Of Otterville, Syracuse, Sedalia, and Versailles
For sending in volunteers and trucks,
Saving Laputa from total apocalypse.
Soon, Clem Cranberry, the Ford dealer, swaggers in;
They chew his superior, pretentious ass
For overcrowding his showroom with mopeds.
"Let the good times roll," one chants.
"They went broke at Edsel's place,
So I decided to get into 2-wheel drive,"
He replies, smiling slyly.
From the far end of the table, another chides,
"Ya gonna sell snowmobiles, too,
When winter comes?"
"Now, I just might look into that!"

The air in this converted gas station
Turns crispy as Texas toast;
The group refuses to quit.
Someone taunts, "Mopo, Mopy, Moped Dick."
They all snort and spew,
Speculating on miles per gallon of ethanol.
"Yeh," Clootie the cop adds,
"One chicken can make enough shit in a year
To get ya to Paris and back."
"You bastard," someone else asserts,
"You're really gonna make it hot
On them poor A-rab camel jockeys, ain't ya?"
"It's cheap transportation,"
Cranberry rebuts seriously, defending his territory.
"You sell $100 helmets with 'em too?" another reproves.
"Sure . . . but they're safe . . .
They're not exactly motorcycles, ya know."
"They ain't exactly tractors neither."
"Hey, boys, give me a *break*!"

"I wonder where ya put the city sticker";
This, after five minutes
Of fierce debate over farming and taxes subsides.
"Let the good times roll";
"Motor awhile, peddle a stretch . . ."
"Hey, maybe you could wear the sticker on your helmet."
"Hey, Mr. Cranberry, sir,
Does a customer get his bikin' shoes from you, too?"
One by one, unceremoniously,
These broad-shouldered, cigarette-smoking,
Seed-capped Laputians take to the sun,
Now dissolving the fog, until only Cranberry,
The last to have arrived, remains,
Like a turkey stewing in its juices.
Bruised but hopeful, he sits musing:
Visions of imported motorbikes
Dominating city streets and country roads,
Ubiquitous as paper clips, fill his mind.
He has the future in his grasp,

But in his inner ear, he still hears their jeering:
"Hey, Cranberry, you traitor,
Did ya get the Pope's blessing on that shipment?"
"Hey, Cranberry, if you'd just get 'T-otas' now,
You'd have it made with all that Jap-crap:
'Laputa presents Cranberry's International Trade Center.'"
"Hey, Cranberry, how many of them moo-peds
You give me for a trade-in on that half-ton
You jewed me into last spring?"
"Hey, Cranberry, maybe Diamond Jim'll follow suit
And dump all *his* gas-guzzlin' Made-in-U.S.A.'s."
"Bastards," he winces, squirming over coffee,
Praying, for the present, anyway,
That he hasn't made a disastrous mistake —
The future may be too far away.
Paying, he leaves and mounts his new steed.
Too lazy to peddle, he gives the starter a pump
And, like the Lone Ranger on a silver scooter,
Sets off up the street, into the sunset.

The Harvesters

The men compare makes of balers and rakes,
Share their agonies of cutting fescue and wheat
In rough, heavy pastures,
Declare the urgency of doing so before the rains
Brush it back, comb it down slick
On the land's scalp.
With indolent vigor they discuss next week's harvest,
Moisture counts reaching 12 to 14,
The imperative that it be dry before storing it in silos.
They deviate momentarily;
"Diamond Jim" Lapedes,
The Chrysler-Plymouth dealer,
Who also just happens to have inherited
The largest farm in the county,
Comprised of more than five thousand acres
He leases out to two dozen real farmers,
From whom he receives thirty percent of their take,
Mentions hunting and fishing,
Leaving Laputa in November for Alaska's upper reaches,
Where ptarmigan, bear, and caribou abound,
Flying into no-man's-land in style
Inside the cab of his air-conditioned Piper "combine,"
Fitted with electric-deicer leading edges,
Flexible wings, and demountable pontoons.

Those gathered in the Capital Café scoff at him,
Guffaw as his incandescent fancy ignites,
Inflates with flatulence his heavier-than-air balloon
Until it hovers above the breakfast table,
Discoloring the room as obscenely as nicotine.
The young bucks among them are jealous as hell.
They'd like to poke holes in his ego
And have him come atumble like the Hindenburg;
Instead, they fantasize about relatives
Fifty years dead, who just as easily
Might have left them their spreads.
Each reasons that the Past was somehow pristine —
If not easier, at least laissez-faired, uninflationary.
*

But hearing about "Diamond Jim's" good fortune
Pisses them off. All they can think of
Is how the fat bastard always brags,
"Success breeds success."
But they know better:
With him, "Greed breeds greed."
Abruptly, the obese blowhard breaks wind;
His balloon, as well as his pants and shirt,
Nearly explodes as he boasts again,
"Eleven hunderd bales from one field ain't hay."
Their envious nodding fails to knot his nozzle;

Instead, he lifts to newer heights,
Drifts on his own winds aloft
To distances the others have never cared to visit,
His reminiscing: "Who woulda ever dreamed
That a humble farmer like me'd
Ever of owned a half-a-million-dollar home
And drive a Designer Series Lincoln
The five miles from County Road T
Into the Capital Café each morning and back,
Change from Slackeaze trousers
To bibs, boots, and seed cap
With 'Funk's G-Hybrid' label on the front
And 'Laputa Golf & Gun Club' on the back?
Who woulda ever believed
That a sod kicker like me'd
Be able to look outta every door
As far as the horizon goes
And know that a flat thirty percent
Of every damn thing he sees,
Corn, sorghum, soybeans, and wheat,
Belongs to him and his wife, Eunice,
Not to mention every clod of the very dirt itself?
Who woulda ever thought I'd see the day
When you young snots'd be lookin' up to me?"

By now, his captive audience,
Instead of applauding with tacit acquiescence
Or egging him on with muffled chuckling,
Begins to leave, one by one by one,
Without so much as bidding him adieu
Or, less formally, extending him a "Screw you"
Or "See you soon, fat ass."
A few, who would normally malinger anyway
For lack of anything better to do —
Laputa's one cop, the mortician,
The editor of the town's "green sheet" newspaper
(A bimonthly journal of ads,
With a sprinkling of local obits and social events),
The wino, the idiot, and the one-armed Vietnam vet —
Remain attentive to his airy soliloquy,
Squealing like pigs, giggling like schoolgirls,
As if his ode to himself has no end.
No one knows, though — certainly not "Diamond Jim" —
That come this November,
After collecting all two dozen of his thirty percents,
Just at the height of the ptarmigan season,
He too will be leaving this elite group
Unexpectedly,
Death having had its most successful harvest as well.

Truckers

5 a.m.'s in Laputa, Mo.,
Are as pitch black
As the inside of a tight fist.

Two dark phantoms
Hover over the steaming, hissing engine
Of their tractor-trailer,

Then, disgustedly, against their better judgment,
Enter the opaque Capital Café.
Abruptly, all the regulars

Disappear behind a two-way mirror
Of white silence.
Both Negro drivers, huddled in a booth,

Crowd the filled room's emptiness;
Hastily they choke down eggs,
Gulp from Fate's bitter cup,

Pay, then flee, like twin Moseses,
Between the parted waters
Of an exceedingly impatient Red Sea.

Disciples Gather at the Farmers' Lyceum

Twelve garrulous disciples contemplate Fate
Around three connected breakfast tables
Haloed with a thick cigarette-smoke inversion,
Formulate political theory
Conforming to Draco, Hadrian, Machiavelli,
Hobbes, Locke, and "Tricky Dick" Nixon,
Affirm the merits of heresy and ethnic bias
In private enterprise,
Debate the values of farmland,
The wisdom of floating municipal bonds below prime,
Using Funk's G-Hybrid, Phister, or Pioneer seeds.

Spontaneously combusting grain elevators,
John Deere, Case, Allis-Chalmers, and Ford tractors,
Shortages of cornfed, antibiotically inoculated beef
And poultry pumped and plumped with steroids,
Prices of soybeans and pork bellies,
Arable acres, stock investments,
And fluctuations in each of these volatile markets
Become the fodder-, chaff-, and grist-catalysts
For epithets, expletives, rhetorical exclamations,
And every other hortatory form of oratory
Beginning with "By God!" and ending with "Hot damn!"

These ethical men cajole each other
About going to Alaska or Cocoa Beach for the winter,
Letting the local Ford dealer
Sell them everything except mopeds,
Feeding cows on milo,
And diverting surplus wheat to the Russian commies.
They ruminate on Mayor Daley's reelection,
A President suckling at Congress' teat,
How far the mercury's dropped in the past minute,
And what they'll do for entertainment
With fields too wet to plow.

When they finally disperse, a wide silence,
Like water undammed from a reservoir,
Inundates the space he, Nate Rosenbloom, occupies.
His mind drowns in such an abrupt deprivation
Of stimulating human intercourse For almost an hour,
He gazes out at tourists navigating the rain
And dreams of the Factory Outlet Mall at the Lake,
Which will soon drain the last drops of local pride
From these disciples of high finance and political theory,
These sons-of-the-sod philosophers,
Who have no idea he too has a messianic calling, of sorts.

Miss Missouri

"With all this cold we've had lately,
The sickle will shatter them beans sure.
Too damn much rain,
Frost too early — Jeez Christ!
Still yet, anyways,
I reckon I'll make a hunderd fifty to the acre."
"Anything goin' on at the Golf & Gun today?"
"Be damned if I know."
"State mowin' the roads again this afternoon?"
"Yeh, 29 and 222,
Routes NN, A, both BBs,
K, and T down to Versailles and Bunceton."
"Why in hell does the state mow in the fall?"
"I bet they'll plow snow next summer, too."

"Say, fellas, you been watchin' over at Syracuse?"
"Oh, you mean that porno movie
Them French guys is makin'?"
"Yeh, they're callin' it *Miss Missouri*."
"I hear they got a bunch of hot girls."
"Yeh, and Paul Newman, too."
"How come *they* get that movie company
And all Laputa gets is Homecomin' this Saturday
And Butterfield Stage Days a coupla weeks ago?"
Someone pumps the waitress, Helen,
For more info about the movie.
"I hear Brando's gonna be flown in for weekend shots."
"Yeh, and who's gonna play Miss Missouri — Jane Fonda?"
"Who?" "Who?" "Who?"

Three different voices rise from below seed caps
In unadulterated ignorance.
"Christ," Helen shrugs, frowning in disbelief.
"Well, why didn't they pick Laputa
If what they wanted was a *real* old town?
Shit, all they'd have to do'd be drive downtown;
We got buildings still bein' used
More rickety than that roadside garage
*

They chose for the breakdown scene."
"Yeh, but Syracuse is smack-dab on the highway,
And what's more, we don't need another whore
With this new crop of high-school sluts we got."
One by one, the voices unravel;
The congregation winnows to two farmers

Reiterating their immediate crisis:
Cutting beans before the next frost scorches their harvest.
But as though someone has laced their coffee
With sodium pentothal, both focus again
On the French movie crew over at Syracuse,
Shaping universal truths from their prurient fantasies.
Helen proffers the brewpot;
Thrusting their cups upward, as in a collective toast,
They draw her salaciously into their conversation.
"Helen, how's 'bout the three of us
Goin' over and auditionin' to be extras?"
"Yeh, we could be them grease monkeys
Who just happen to be handy at midnight
To fix Miss Missouri's busted transmission."

"Yeh, and who do you think I could play?"
She snickers, rubbing her hip
Against "Hosey" Lovegarten's outstretched arm.
"Ah, shit, Helen,
You could just be your ol' sweet self
And you'd knock 'em dead."
"Oh, sure — you mean do it cold turkey,
Without even rehearsin' my lines?"
"What lines? What they got in mind for Miss Missouri
Don't need no practice;
Fact is, that particular scene
Don't even need no subtitles."
"On second thought," Lovegarten adds, leering,
"Maybe we'd *better* practice . . . out back."

Vigilantes

Even at this early morning hour in December,
Laputa's dependable vigilantes are awake,
Having coffee, ham steaks, and eggs at the Capital Café
Before manning the watchtowers.
Among their most pressing topics of discussion
Are the bone-chattering cold weather,
Slick fields inaccessible to tractor and half-ton,
And frozen ponds denying their water to cows.

As soon as an unusual lull intrudes
Through a space their mutual chewing provides,
One sets free into the momentary clearing
A joke-snake from his cage of bigotries.
"Did you hear about the nigger boy
Who found a gold shoe? When he shined it,
A genie appeared and gave him two wishes.
'I'se alweez wanted to be white.' 'Granted!'
'I'se alweez wanted to have a pile of money
Without workin' for it.' The genie stops,
Thinks awhile, then says, 'You're black again!'"
The self-deputized P.B.P.C.[1] guffaw,
Nod in all-knowing agreement.

Taking the stage after another brief hiatus,
During which Helen serves their fourth round of coffee
And two more platters of gravy biscuits,
Police Chief Clootie Butcher,
Laputa's one and only duly elected keeper of the peace,
Known to most as "the town cop,"
Breaks into a protracted peroration
On a caper that occurred late last night,
To which he was called from the dead of sleep.
"Boys, you wouldn'a believed who I caught red-handed,
Nekkid as newborn brush apes,
Fuckin' their brains out."
"Who, Clootie, who?" the entire group demands of him.

---

[1] Protectors of Benevolent & Pious Causes

Cracking his knuckles, stroking his stubble,
Scratching his crotch, belching twice,
Picking his nose, removing his cap,
And wiping his sweaty forehead with his tie,
His drawn-out pause taunting them mercilessly,
He finally whispers his report:
"*Helen* and some coon I ain't never seed before,
Prob'ly from over past Boonville!"
"Whad'ya do then, Cloot?"
"They was goin' at it like two zebras in heat;
I had to pry 'em loose with a crowbar,
And you shoulda seed that jigaboo run for his life —
He's prob'ly back in Africa with his tribe by now!

"But I got his drawers, shoes, and socks, alright,
Locked up as prime evidence
In case he ever shows his black ass in Laputa again,
Where that kinda mixed shit just don't go."
Innocent to their private confidings,
Helen, arms raised high, a coffeepot in each hand,
Thrusts herself in and out,
Refilling their cups with hot draught.
After she disappears into the kitchen,
Clootie pulls from a pocket inside his jacket
Exhibits **D** and **E** from the scene of the crime:
Helen's skimpy, red-lace panties and bra.
Brandishing them, he sets the men aquiver.

This pack of hyenas remains so distracted by its laughter
That none sees her reenter their area.
She recognizes at once the lingerie they're passing around,
Realizes their hilarity is at her expense.
To achieve parity, she hustles to the kitchen,
Returns with a tray she puts on a rack by their table,
Then begins grabbing platters of steaming gravy biscuits
She "accidentally" dumps in their laps.
*

"Say, boys, I don't know if any of yous noticed,
But I ain't got nothin' on 'neath my clothes —
Seems I done run clean outta undies."
Stunned, shouting, clutching their painfully hot crotches,
All focus on Helen Bone's diaphanous uniform

As they rush disgustedly from the café,
Heading home to change their sullied drawers
Before assuming once more
Their monumental duties of maintaining Laputa's integrity.
After the room's been cleared,
Leaving silence to clean up the leftovers, reset the table,
Helen picks up and pockets her "tip":
One gravy-stained set of intimate apparel.

KKK: Ozymandias Klavern, Laputa, Mo.

Farmers lumbering in from their frozen farms
Like bears waking prematurely from hibernation;
Mailman in gray, beneath fur hat;
Parts manager at the Ford dealership;
Mustached construction boys in union caps
And mud-encrusted work boots;
Bartender from Joe and Ginger's Tropicana;
Road-crew supervisor and assorted hands;
Bank president; Judas Shoe factory foreman;
Loss-Prevention Specialist/clerk
For Ebert's Five-and-Dime;
Funeral parlor director;
Laputa's police force of one;
Lone Sanitation Engineer;
City attorney/barber/notary public;
Half a dozen stray cats and mangy mutts
From outposts in a ten-mile radius . . .

All converge on town tonight,
In the Capital Café's trap-doored basement,
To take strength from their monthly rites,
Don the dress of their Klan-destine profession,
White robes and hoods,
Then gather torches, cans of kerosene, and makeshift crosses
For the purpose of reasserting their suzerainty
Over intruders of all persuasions:
Atheists, dagos, jigaboos, fags, dykes,
Commies, Catholics, spics, kikes,
And other racial, religious, sexual, and political "preverts,"
Some not yet even named, let alone known to them,
Despite reports they've been getting lately from TV
That all mayhem and chaos has broken loose
Not only in Jeff City, Sedalia, and Columbia
But on their very doorstep,
In the streets of Brazito, Versailles, and Syracuse.

➙

Within the next few hours,
These pillars of the community,
Protectors of God's *real* Word,
Divine practitioners of Applied Christianity,
Mostly Baptists at heart
(With a few miscellaneous Protestants thrown in),
Will have sparked the dark, left their sinister mark
On a dozen yards, barns, storefronts, trucks,
Whose unsuspecting owners, for weeks on end,
Will cringe in their own piss,
Wondering when the next nocturnal scourge
Of wizards, knights, and dragons,
Imperial and exalted emissaries of Satan, will occur.
Worse, sharing the same streets of Laputa,
They'll be forced to speak on a first-name basis
With those they know full well profess:
"Look upon our mighty works, ye Meek, and despair!"

Clayton Ladue at the Café des Beaux-Arts

No Botticellian *La Primavera*,
Sprawling peasant scene
From prematurely surreal Bosch,
Nor serene, 15th-century Flemish rendering
With placid, pristine stream
Meandering to its vanishing point
In the mythical distance gyved by a castle
Probing divinely skyward is this lithograph,

But rather two four-by-eight cardboard posters
Redolent of Ebert's Five-and-Dime
That adorn the Capital Café's booth-lined wall,
Their warped, vertical seams
Obviously mismatched
At the juncture where separate horizons
Run past each other
On endlessly bending parallel tracks.

In this scape, the time of day is dusk,
Emblazoned in mauve, fuchsia,
And gaudy gradations of hazy yellow and orange;
The bland scene repeats an ageless cliché:
A calm, boatless ocean
Surmounted by an even more tranquil sky,
The whole enclosed on the left side
By a lone palm tree

Growing out of an invisible beach,
Climbing in slender sinuosity
Toward the upper border,
Its frond tops cropped arbitrarily.
For a moment, his tired eyes
Superimpose a Renaissance maiden, on a half shell,
Rising out of the water,
Thighs, "V," belly, nipples dripping sensually;

His libido populates the nonexistent sands
Just below the lower edge
With myriad sun-screened, massaged bodies
Bathing in naked obeisance to the Sun,
To the great god Lust.
Fleetingly, Fancy persuades him
He can actually reach fabled Cathay
If only focus can be maintained.

Suddenly Helen, the Capital's brainless waitress,
Undistinguished save for her furtive smile,
Disturbs his reverie by brushing his ear
As she places eggs and toast on the table.
Paying, tipping her twenty-five dollars,
And glancing again at the tasteless seascape mural,
He realizes how art can initiate, not just imitate, life —
Like later tonight at the Lorelei.

Butterfield Stage Pub

Blue- or green-felt, long-billed seed caps
Hover two feet above each tabletop.
Somewhere beneath this aura,
Gnarled field-faces
And merchant-frowns from downtown's single street
Wade cow-solemn and pace civically
Through spacious depths,
Debating row-crop, feedlot speculation,
The high school's bankrupt condition,
"Red" Brewster's suicide this past April
After learning his wife left him for a lesbian,
"Diamond Jim" Lapedes' recent death,
Pollution from the Judas Shoe factory,
And the cost of hogs per pound in Chicago and K.C.

Despite its garishly bright vinyl floor tiles,
Fake brick, wallpaper depicting thousands of retrievers
With ducks dangling from their mouths,
And simulated, brown-stained,
Boxed-in ceiling beams of one-by-six boards
Reminiscent of an Elizabethan dining hall,
Which form a Tudor-like sore thumb
Amidst the bucolic squalor of this overgrown hamlet,
None has found it necessary
To differentiate between this newly built eating place
They already derisively call the "Butterball"
And the converted gas station,
The Capital Café,
From which they've lately, for now, defected.

However, they know one thing for certain:
Three hundred cups of coffee,
Eighty plates of homemade gravy biscuits and hash browns,
Forty platters of sausage patties,
And five dozen orders of ham steaks and Texas toast
Served up every morning for ten years straight
Won't even begin to pay the monthly lease
Of its new proprietor, "Sherm" Sterneck,
*

Just over from Sedalia
With the hope of making a quick killing
Stealing away the Capital's regulars
On unfounded rumors that its owners,
Cecil and Ella May Scroggins,
Might be moving away to Arizona or somewhere.

Strangely, it's as though nothing's changed.
After all, the boys could just as easily chew the fat
In the Union Labor Hall,
Joe and Ginger's Tropicana Lounge,
The stockroom of Sandman's Hardware,
Or, for that matter,
In any one of the twenty-three sleazy "suites"
Of Sneed's Lorelei Motel at the edge of town,
Where they've all stayed anyway
On a pay-as-you-go-and-come basis
More nights than any of them would care to admit
Even in this "men's only" quilting bee.
Truth is, they don't give a shit where they sit
So long as someone else's payin' for it.

Workers of the Word, Unite!

To the scraggly-faced fathers of today's regulars,
The Capital Café/gas station
Was a welcome oasis;
They came around 5 each a.m. to seed the dirt,
Again at noon to fertilize rumors,
And returned at dusk to bale the harvested gossip
Their base mortality required for sustenance.

But last week, four months late,
The descendants of those pioneering fat-chewers
Expressed their condolences on its passing
By sending plastic flowers and baskets of waxed fruit
To the town's newest institution of haute cuisine:
"Sherm" Sterneck's Butterfield Stage Pub,
A latter-day Crystal Palace
Of recessed ceiling, four-bulb, fluorescent fixtures,
Fake brick, particle-board beams,
And Penney's mail-order, ten-dollar-a-roll
"Scenes from the Great Outdoors" wallpaper,
To which the scraggly-faced sons of the original regulars
Now come to monitor sunrise, sunshine, sunset,
Old Testament rain, sleet by the sheet,
Tractor-deep snow, pea-soup fog,
Softballs of hail, hellfire heat, Biblical drought,
And plagues of grasshoppers or cicadas,
Weddings, elopements, baptisms, adulteries, divorces,
Sicknesses, suicides, funerals,
Bankruptcies, foreclosures, auctions,
Sightings of faggot, lesbian, and nigger atrocities,
Not to mention other egregious "preversions"
Among Laputa's putative leading citizens and bums,

And, most significantly, through their omniscient eyes,
To advise God Himself
On the state of the Universal Human Condition
By keeping Him apprised
Of the daily doings of their fellow Laputians
And by not betraying the covenant duly entrusted to them
To love thy neighbor and never profane His name.
                              Amen.

Biographical Note

Louis Daniel Brodsky was born in St. Louis, Missouri, in 1941, where he attended St. Louis Country Day School. After earning a B.A., magna cum laude, at Yale University in 1963, he received an M.A. in English from Washington University in 1967 and an M.A. in Creative Writing from San Francisco State University the following year.

Mr. Brodsky is the author of twenty volumes of poetry, five of which have been translated for French publication by Éditions Gallimard. His poems have appeared in *Harper's*, *Southern Review*, *Texas Quarterly*, *National Forum*, *American Scholar*, *Kansas Quarterly*, Ball State University's *Forum*, and *Literary Review*, as well as in five editions of the *Anthology of Magazine Verse and Yearbook of American Poetry*.

Also available from **Time Being Books**®

LOUIS DANIEL BRODSKY

You Can't Go Back, Exactly
The Thorough Earth
Four and Twenty Blackbirds Soaring
Mississippi Vistas: Volume One of *A Mississippi Trilogy*
Falling from Heaven: Holocaust Poems of a Jew and a Gentile
    (with William Heyen)
Forever, for Now: Poems for a Later Love
Mistress Mississippi: Volume Three of *A Mississippi Trilogy*
A Gleam in the Eye: Poems for a First Baby
Gestapo Crows: Holocaust Poems
The Capital Café: Poems of Redneck, U.S.A.

HARRY JAMES CARGAS (Editor)

Telling the Tale: A Tribute to Elie Wiesel on the Occasion of His
    65th Birthday — Essays, Reflections, and Poems

ROBERT HAMBLIN

From the Ground Up: Poems of One Southerner's Passage
    to Adulthood

WILLIAM HEYEN

Erika: Poems of the Holocaust
Falling from Heaven: Holocaust Poems of a Jew and a Gentile
    (with Louis Daniel Brodsky)
Pterodactyl Rose: Poems of Ecology
Ribbons: The Gulf War — A Poem

TED HIRSCHFIELD
German Requiem: Poems of the War and the Atonement of a Third Reich Child

VIRGINIA V. JAMES HLAVSA
Waking October Leaves: Reanimations of a Small-Town Girl

RODGER KAMENETZ
The Missing Jew: New and Selected Poems

NORBERT KRAPF
Somewhere in Southern Indiana: Poems of Midwestern Origins

JOSEPH MEREDITH
Hunter's Moon: Poems from Boyhood to Manhood

TIME BEING BOOKS®
POETRY IN SIGHT AND SOUND

FOR OUR FREE CATALOG OR TO ORDER

(800) 331-6605 Monday through Friday
8 a.m. to 4 p.m. Central time
FAX: (314) 432-7939